Series Editor

Lisa Firth

First published by Independence

The Studio, High Green

Great Shelford

Cambridge CB22 5EG

England

© Independence 2010

British Library Cataloguing in Publication Data

Tobacco and health. -- (Issues ; v. 188)

1. Smoking.

I. Series II. Firth, Lisa.

362.2'96-dc22

ISBN-13: 978 1 86168 539 1

Printed in Great Britain

MWL Print Group Ltd

CONTENTS

OTHER TITLES IN THE ISSUES SERIES

For more on these titles, visit: www.independence.co.uk

EXPLORING THE ISSUES

Photocopiable study guides to accompany the above publications. Each four-page A4 guide provides a variety of discussion points and other activities to suit a wide range of ability levels and interests.

A note on critical evaluation

Because the information reprinted here is from a number of different sources, readers should bear in mind the origin of the text and whether the source is likely to have a particular bias when presenting information (just as they would if undertaking their own research). It is hoped that, as you read about the many aspects of the issues explored in this book, you will critically evaluate the information presented. It is important that you decide whether you are being presented with facts or opinions. Does the writer give a biased or an unbiased report? If an opinion is being expressed, do you agree with the writer?

Tobacco and Health offers a useful starting point for those who need convenient access to information about the many issues involved. However, it is only a starting point. Following each article is a URL to the relevant organisation's website, which you may wish to visit for further information.

Chapter 1

Smoking among adults, 2008

Trends in the prevalence of cigarette smoking.

The overall prevalence of smoking among the adult population was the same in 2008 as it was in 2007 at 21 per cent.

The prevalence of cigarette smoking fell substantially in the 1970s and the early 1980s, from 45 per cent in 1974 to 35 per cent in 1982. The rate of decline then slowed, with prevalence falling by only about one percentage point every two years until 1994, after which it levelled out at about 27 per cent before resuming a slow decline in the 2000s.

It should be noted that during periods when the prevalence of smoking in the general population is changing little, upward and downward movements in survey estimates are to be expected, and this can make the detection of trends over a short period difficult.

Throughout the period in which the GHS has been monitoring cigarette smoking, prevalence has been higher among men than women but in 2008 the difference between men and women was not statistically significant. In 2008, 22 per cent of men and 21 per cent of women were cigarette smokers.

The difference in prevalence between men and women has decreased considerably since the 1970s. In 1974, for example, 51 per cent of men smoked cigarettes, compared with 41 per cent of women. The narrowing of the gender gap is mainly due to a combination of two factors.

First, there is a cohort effect resulting from the fact that smoking became common among men several decades before it did among women. In the 1970s there was a fall in the proportion of women aged 60 and over who had never smoked regularly.

Second, men are more likely than women to have given up smoking cigarettes. It should be noted, however, that this difference conceals the fact that some men who give up smoking cigarettes remain smokers (by continuing to smoke cigars and pipes). This is very rare among women who stop smoking cigarettes.

The proportion of respondents saying that they had never smoked did not change significantly between 2007 and 2008. The proportion of women who reported being ex-smokers did not change but the proportion of men ex-smokers rose from 28 per cent to 30 per cent.

Over the last 30 years there have been falls in the prevalence of smoking in all age groups. Since the survey began, the GHS has shown considerable fluctuation in prevalence rates among those aged 16 to 19, particularly if young men and young women are considered separately. However, this is mainly because of the relatively small sample size in this age group and occurred within a pattern of overall decline in smoking prevalence in this age group from 31 per cent in 1998 to 22 per cent in 2008. Since the early 1990s the prevalence of cigarette smoking has been higher among those aged 20 to 34 than among those in other age groups. This continued to be the case in 2008 when 30 per cent of the 20 to 24 age group and 27 per cent of the 25 to 34 age group were smokers. Prevalence continued to be lowest among adults aged 60 and over at 13 per cent.

Cigarette smoking and marital status

The prevalence of cigarette smoking varies considerably according to marital status. The groups with the highest proportion of smokers were cohabiting men (33 per cent), cohabiting women (30 per cent) and single women (29 per cent). Smoking prevalence was much lower among married people (16 per cent) than among those in any of the three other marital status categories (single, cohabiting, and widowed, divorced or separated). This is not explained by the association between age and marital status (for example, married people and those who are widowed, divorced or separated are older, on average, than single people). In every age group except the youngest, married people were less likely to be smokers than were other respondents (although in the 60 plus age group due to the small size of the cohabiting group it is not significantly different from the married group). For example, among those aged 25 to 34, 34 per cent of those who were single and 31 per cent of those who were cohabiting were smokers, compared with only 19 per cent of those who were married.

Cigarette smoking and socio-economic classification

The National Statistics Socio-economic Classification (NS-SEC), which was introduced in 2001, does not allow categories to be collapsed into broad non-manual and manual groupings. So, since the *Cancer Plan* targets for England relate particularly to those in the manual socio-economic groups, the old socio-economic groupings have been recreated for this report in Table 1.6*. As a result of the new occupation coding, the classifications are not exactly the same, and comparisons with previous years should be made with caution.

The GHS has consistently shown striking differences in the prevalence of cigarette smoking in relation to socio-economic group, with smoking being considerably more prevalent among those in manual groups than among those in non-manual groups. In the 1970s, 1980s and 1990s, the prevalence of cigarette smoking fell more sharply among those in non-manual than in manual groups, so that differences between the groups became proportionately greater.

In the period between 1998 and 2008 smoking continued to fall more quickly in the non-manual group than in the manual group. In the non-manual group smoking fell by a quarter over this period while in the manual group it fell by a fifth. In England in 2008, 27 per cent of those in manual groups were cigarette smokers, compared with 33 per cent in 1998. In the non-manual group 16 per cent were smokers in 2008 compared with 22 per cent in 1998. In 1998 smoking prevalence in the manual group was 1.5 times that in the non-manual group. In 2008 smoking prevalence in the manual group was approximately 1.7 times that in the non-manual group.

However, caution is advisable when making comparisons over this period: the recreated socio-economic groups may have been affected by the change from head of household to household reference person as the basis for assessing socio-economic group, and by revisions to the way in which occupation is coded.

Table 1.7* shows similar trends in England since 2001 using the new socio-economic classification (NS-SEC) of the household reference person. It was noted earlier that there is a PSA target to reduce the prevalence of smoking among those in households classified as routine or manual to 26 per cent or lower by 2010. Over the period 2001 to 2008, the prevalence of cigarette smoking fell by four percentage points among those in routine and manual households (from 33 per cent to 29 per cent), and by six percentage points among those in intermediate households (from 27 per cent to 21 per cent). Prevalence fell by five percentage points among those in managerial and professional households (from 19 per cent in 2001 to 14 per cent in 2008). Smoking is now twice as common in routine and manual households as it is in managerial and professional households (29 per cent compared to 14 per cent).

The prevalence of cigarette smoking in Great Britain in 2008 in relation to the eight- and three-category versions of NS-SEC is shown in Table 1.8*. As was the case with the socio-economic groupings used previously, there were striking differences between the various classes. Prevalence was lowest among those in higher professional households and those in large employer and higher managerial households (12 per cent) and highest, at 32 per cent, among those whose household reference person was in a routine occupation.

Cigarette smoking and economic activity

Those who were economically active were more likely to smoke than those who were not, but this is largely explained by the lower prevalence of smoking among those aged 60 and over, who form the majority of economically inactive people.

Prevalence was highest among economically inactive people aged 16 to 59: 28 per cent of this group were smokers, compared with 23 per cent of economically active people and only 13 per cent of economically inactive people aged 60 and over. Prevalence was particularly high among economically inactive people aged 16 to 59 whose last job was a routine or manual one, 42 per cent of whom were cigarette smokers.

It should be noted that these figures refer to the socio-economic classification of the current or last job of the individual whereas the figures in the previous section refer to the socio-economic classification of the current or last job of the household reference person.

Age started smoking

The White Paper *Smoking Kills* noted that people who start smoking at an early age are more likely than other smokers to smoke for a long period of time and more likely to die from a smoking-related disease.

About two-thirds of respondents who were either current smokers or who had smoked regularly at some time in their lives had started smoking before they were 18. Almost two-fifths had started smoking regularly before the age of 16 even though it has been illegal to sell cigarettes to people under 16 since 1908 and has recently become illegal to sell cigarettes to people less than 18 years of age. Men were more likely than women to have started smoking before they were 16 (40 per cent of men who had ever smoked regularly, compared with 37 per cent of women in 2008).

Since the early 1990s there has been an increase in the proportion of women taking up smoking before the age of 16. In 1992, 28 per cent of women who had ever smoked started before they were 16. In 2008 this rose to 37 per cent. There has been little change since 1992 in the proportion of men who had ever smoked who had started smoking regularly before the age of 16.

About two-thirds of respondents who were current smokers or had smoked regularly at some time had started smoking before they were 18

As the GHS has shown in previous years, there was an association between age started smoking regularly and socio-economic classification based on the current or last job of the household reference person. In managerial and professional households, 32 per cent of smokers had started smoking before they were 16, compared with 44 per cent of those in routine and manual households.

Current heavy smokers were more likely than light or ex-smokers to have started smoking at an early age. Of those smoking 20 or more cigarettes a day, 47 per cent started smoking regularly before they were 16, compared with 40 per cent of those currently smoking fewer than ten cigarettes a day.

Cigarette consumption

The overall decline in smoking prevalence since the mid-1970s has been due to a fall in the proportions of both 'light to moderate' smokers (defined as fewer than 20 cigarettes per day) and heavy smokers (20 cigarettes or more per day). The proportion of adults smoking on average 20 or more cigarettes a day among men fell from 26 per cent in 1974 to seven per cent in 2008, and from 13 per cent to five per cent among women. Over the same period the proportion smoking fewer than 20 per day fell from 25 per cent to 15 per cent for men and from 28 per cent to 15 per cent for women.

In all age groups, respondents were much more likely to be 'light to moderate' than heavy smokers, the difference was most pronounced among those aged under 35. For example, 22 per cent of men and 22 per cent of women aged 25 to 34 were 'light to moderate' smokers in 2008, and only seven per cent and four per cent respectively were heavy smokers.

The overall reported number of cigarettes smoked per male and female smoker has changed little since the early 1980s. As in previous years, male smokers smoked slightly more cigarettes a day on average than female smokers: in 2008, men smoked on average 14 cigarettes a day, compared with 13 for women. Among both men and women smokers, cigarette consumption varied by age. The highest average was 16 cigarettes a day among men in the 50 to 59 age group although the difference between this group and the 35 to 49 and 60 and over age groups was not statistically significant.

GHS reports have consistently shown cigarette consumption levels to be higher among male and female smokers in manual socio-economic groups than among those in non-manual groups. A similar pattern is evident in relation to NS-SEC. In 2008, smokers in households where the household reference person was in a routine or manual occupation smoked an average of 14 cigarettes a day, compared with 11 a day for those in managerial or professional households.

Cigar and pipe smoking

A decline in the prevalence of pipe and cigar smoking among men has been evident since the survey began, with most of the reduction occurring in the 1970s and 1980s.

In 2008 only two per cent of men smoked at least one cigar a month, compared with 34 per cent in 1974. Only a small number of women smoked cigars in 1974, and since 1978 the percentages have been scarcely measurable on the GHS.

Only one per cent of men in 2008 said they smoked a pipe, and they were almost all aged 50 and over. Cigar smoking is slightly more common among men aged 30 and over than it is among men aged under 30.

26 January 2010
* Tables can be found in the full version of the report at www.statistics.gov.uk/downloads/theme_compendia/ GLF08/GLFSmoking&DrinkingAmongAdults2008.pdf

⇨ The above information is an extract from the Office for National Statistics document *Smoking and drinking among adults 2008* and is reprinted with permission.

Tobacco

Information from Hope UK.

Many adults are concerned about young people's involvement with illegal drugs, but the overwhelming majority of young people identify correctly that tobacco and alcohol are the greatest drug-related dangers (Ofsted report as recorded in the *Guardian*, 12 April 2007).

Every year, around 114,000 smokers in the UK die from smoking-related causes. About half of all regular cigarette smokers will eventually be killed by their addiction (www.ash.org.uk).

What is in a cigarette?

You've heard of nicotine but, when it comes to health, that's the least of your worries. Each cigarette contains around 4,000 chemicals, many of which are known to be toxic. Here are a few of the nasties you'll be inhaling in every drag:

⇨ Acetone – widely used as a solvent, for example in nail polish remover.

⇨ Ammonia – found in cleaning fluids.

⇨ Arsenic – a deadly poison, used in insecticides.

⇨ Formaldehyde – used to preserve dead bodies.

⇨ Cadmium – a highly poisonous metal used in batteries.

⇨ Shellac – becomes a wood varnish when mixed with a form of alcohol.

⇨ Benzene – used as a solvent in fuel and chemical production.

⇨ Cyanide – a deadly poison.

⇨ Tar – a mixture of chemicals (including formaldehyde, arsenic and cyanide). About 70% of the tar is left in smokers' lungs, causing a range of serious lung conditions.

⇨ Carbon monoxide (CO) – an odourless, tasteless and poisonous gas; makes breathing more difficult as it combines with the blood that carries oxygen around the body. Up to 15% of a smoker's blood may be carrying CO instead of oxygen, making the heart work harder, and potentially leading to coronary heart disease and circulation problems (www.nosmokingday.org.uk).

Smoking facts

⇨ Over 80% of smokers start as teenagers.

⇨ In England one-fifth of 15-year-olds are regular smokers: 16% of boys and 24% of girls.

⇨ It is illegal to sell cigarettes to any person under the age of 18. (www.ash.org.uk).

⇨ Smoking is the single greatest avoidable risk factor for cancer; in the UK, it is the cause of more than a quarter (29%) of all deaths from cancer and has killed an estimated six million people over the last 50 years.

⇨ Smoking causes 90% of lung cancers in men and up to 86% of cases in women in developed countries (http://info.cancerresearchuk.org/cancerstats/causes/lifestyle/tobacco/).

For more information

⇨ www.ash.org.uk

⇨ www.nosmokingday.org.uk

⇨ www.quit.org.uk

Much of the above information relates either to the UK or to England alone. Information about Northern Ireland, Scotland or Wales can be found from:

⇨ Northern Ireland – www.healthpromotionagency.org.uk

⇨ Scotland – www.healthscotland.com

⇨ Welsh Assembly – http://new.wales.gov.uk [and then search for tobacco statistics]

⇨ The above information is reprinted with kind permission from Hope UK. Visit www.hopeuk.org for more information.

HOPE UK

Smoking and your lungs

Information from the British Lung Foundation.

Cigarette smoke

Cigarette smoke contains many substances which can damage the lungs. The smoke has two parts: tiny solid pieces which contain tar, and the gas, which contains carbon monoxide and nitrogen oxides. Smoking takes these poisonous substances directly into your lungs. The filters in most cigarettes are of some benefit, but they still let most of the harmful chemicals into your lungs.

The dangers of smoking

The tar in cigarette smoke damages cells in the airways of your lungs. Eventually this damage can produce cells that grow uncontrollably – leading to cancer of the lung or voice box (larynx).

Because of this, your body sends protecting cells to your lungs to try and defend them, but cigarette smoke destroys them. The dead cells then release substances that damage the structure of the lung. This leads to Chronic Obstructive Pulmonary Disease (COPD).

Passive smokers inhale smoke breathed in and out by smokers. They also breathe in the smoke from the burning tips of cigarettes

Cigarette smoke also releases substances into your bloodstream that damage other organs. The arteries can be affected in your heart, brain and other places. This can lead to angina, heart attacks, strokes and poor circulation. It also increases your chances of developing cancer in other areas of the body, such as the gullet or bladder.

Passive smoking

Passive smokers inhale smoke breathed in and out by smokers. They also breathe in the smoke from the burning tips of cigarettes. This smoke contains more of the harmful chemicals than the smoke which has passed through the cigarette filter.

Passive smoking often troubles non-smokers, especially if they have asthma or other lung problems.

Children growing up with parents who smoke are more likely to develop lung problems. The risk of sudden death in young children is also increased when their parents smoke. There is a small increase in the risk of lung cancer in non-smokers who are in close contact with smokers for a long time.

Smoking in Britain

In March 2006 a ban on smoking in all public places and workplaces began in Scotland.

A similar ban began in Wales and Northern Ireland during April 2007 and began in England on 1 July 2007.

Despite all the problems resulting from cigarette smoking, many people continue to smoke – around 25 per cent of all adults in the United Kingdom. Most smokers start as teenagers. Most adult smokers want at some time to quit.

It is becoming less socially acceptable to smoke and the number of adults is gradually going down. Unfortunately the number of young girls taking up smoking is increasing. Children brought up in non-smoking homes are much less likely to take up the habit.

The benefits of stopping

The sooner you stop, the less likely it is that your lungs and other organs will be damaged. Symptoms such as coughing can get better within days or weeks. If COPD has started to develop, stopping smoking will prevent further damage. Continuing to smoke causes a steady increase in shortness of breath. This limits your activity and increases the risks of lung and heart failure. It is never too late to think about stopping.

The risk of lung cancer increases the more you smoke, and the longer you smoke. Once you stop, the risk of lung cancer starts to go down. After ten years off cigarettes, the risk is halved compared to the risk if you had continued smoking.

Whilst some people go through life unaffected by smoking, millions do not. Too many people think 'It will never happen to me' – until they develop cancer or have their first heart attack.

Stopping smoking

Stopping smoking can be very difficult, but many smokers find it easier than expected. More and more people are managing to quit the habit. Most smokers are addicted to the nicotine in cigarettes and may have withdrawal symptoms such as craving, irritability, depression and loss of concentration.

The severity of withdrawal symptoms can be reduced by using nicotine replacement therapies (NRT), such as nicotine patches, chewing gum, lozenges, spray, inhalator or tablets. These can provide 'clean' nicotine and are much safer than smoking cigarettes. They should be used for about six weeks, then stopped, and are available from your chemist or on prescription from your GP. Clinical trials have shown that, if you want to stop smoking, using a nicotine product nearly doubles your chance of success.

New drugs are now being developed that help reduce the withdrawal symptoms of stopping. These tablets can be given with nicotine replacement treatments and, like NRT, can double the success rate of smokers who try to stop. These are only available on prescription from your GP, who may also advise you to use them alongside local smoking cessation services. Your GP can advise you on potential side effects.

It is generally a good idea to fix a quit date, rather than gradually reduce your smoking. Tell people around you that you are going to stop, and try to get others at home or work to stop with you. This support network makes it easier when temptation arises!

One concern for smokers is weight gain; smoking suppresses your appetite, so you can avoid gaining weight if you are aware of this, if you take exercise and eat healthily.

People who switch from cigarettes to pipes or cigars gain very little benefit in terms of improved good health. Again, it is better to stop smoking completely.

Many doctors, hospitals and local health authorities run support groups and courses to help. Your GP can tell you what is available locally. Despite the difficulties, more smokers are managing to stop every day. It can be done and you will find very definite benefits in your health and the quality of your life.

⇨ Information from the British Lung Foundation. Visit www.lunguk.org for more.

© British Lung Foundation

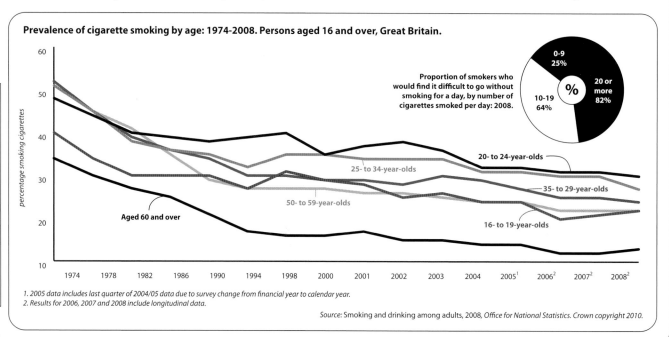

Prevalence of cigarette smoking by age: 1974-2008. Persons aged 16 and over, Great Britain.

Proportion of smokers who would find it difficult to go without smoking for a day, by number of cigarettes smoked per day: 2008.

1. 2005 data includes last quarter of 2004/05 data due to survey change from financial year to calendar year.
2. Results for 2006, 2007 and 2008 include longitudinal data.

Source: Smoking and drinking among adults, 2008, Office for National Statistics. Crown copyright 2010.

Smoking and your heart

How smoking damages your heart and circulation.

Chemicals in cigarette smoke can damage the lining of the coronary arteries. This leads to atherosclerosis – the build-up of fatty material within the walls of the arteries which is the cause of coronary heart disease.

The nicotine in cigarettes stimulates the body to produce adrenaline, which makes the heart beat faster and raises the blood pressure

The carbon monoxide in tobacco smoke is the same type of poisonous gas found in car exhaust fumes. It puts the heart at risk because it deprives the heart of vital oxygen. Oxygen is carried around the body by red blood cells. The oxygen joins onto haemoglobin – the red protein within the red blood cells. However, the carbon monoxide in cigarette smoke also joins onto the haemoglobin, reducing the amount of oxygen that the blood can carry around the body. In some smokers, up to half of the blood can be carrying carbon monoxide instead of oxygen.

Tobacco smoke also has an effect on the sticky particles in the blood called platelets. This makes the blood more likely to clot.

The nicotine in cigarettes stimulates the body to produce adrenaline, which makes the heart beat faster and raises the blood pressure for a short while immediately after smoking. This means that, each time you smoke a cigarette, your heart has to work harder.

It is the tar found in cigarettes that causes cancer. However, if a cigarette is low in tar, it does not necessarily mean that it has less nicotine and carbon monoxide, so low-tar cigarettes can be just as harmful to your heart as regular cigarettes. Also, people who smoke low-tar cigarettes tend to compensate by taking more puffs and inhaling more deeply. Research shows that smokers of 'light' or 'mild' brands of cigarettes are likely to inhale as much tar and nicotine as smokers of regular cigarettes. Just three or four extra puffs on a cigarette can change a low-tar cigarette into a regular-strength cigarette.

Smoking and your heart

⇨ Coronary heart disease is the single most common cause of death in the UK.

⇨ Smoking is one of the major risk factors for coronary heart disease. (A risk factor is something that increases the chance of getting the disease.) Up to 19 in every 100 deaths from coronary heart disease are associated with smoking.

Other risk factors for coronary heart disease are: having high levels of cholesterol in the blood; high blood pressure; physical inactivity; being overweight or obese; diabetes; and having a family history of coronary heart disease.

16 June 2009

⇨ The above information is reprinted with kind permission from the British Heart Foundation. Visit www. bhf.org.uk for more information.

© *British Heart Foundation*

BRITISH HEART FOUNDATION

Tobacco, smoking and cancer: the evidence

This article contains information about the links between smoking and cancer.

Smoking is the single biggest cause of cancer in the world

Experts agree that smoking is the single biggest cause of cancer in the world. Smoking causes over a quarter of cancer deaths in developed countries.

Around half of current smokers will be killed by their habit if they continue to smoke. And 25–40% of smokers will die in middle age.

Smoking causes even more deaths from other respiratory diseases and heart conditions than from cancer. If current trends continue, scientists estimate that tobacco will kill about one billion people in the 21st century.

Smoking greatly increases the risk of lung cancer

Studies from Europe, Japan and North America have shown that nine in ten lung cancers are caused by smoking. In 2002, lung cancer killed around 33,600 people – about one person every 15 minutes.

Tobacco smoke was first shown to cause lung cancer in 1950. This study found that people who smoked 15–24 cigarettes a day had 26 times the lung cancer risk of non-smokers. And people who smoked less than 15 cigarettes a day still had eight times the lung cancer risk of non-smokers.

After these first results came out, UK scientists began a large study of smoking in British doctors, which Cancer Research UK has helped to fund. This British Doctors' Study has provided much of our current knowledge about the dangers of smoking.

The people with the highest lung cancer risks are those who:

⇨ smoke the most cigarettes per day;

⇨ smoke over long periods of time; and

⇨ start smoking young.

We cannot exactly calculate a person's lung cancer risk based on how many cigarettes they smoke or the number of years they have been a smoker. But studies have shown that lung cancer risk is greatest among those who smoke the most cigarettes over the longest period of time.

The length of time spent smoking seems to be the more important of these two factors. The British Doctors' Study found that people who had smoked for 45 years had 100 times the lung cancer risk of people who had smoked for 15 years, regardless of whether they smoked heavily or

moderately. And smoking one packet a day for 40 years is about eight times more dangerous than smoking two packets a day for 20 years.

Even light or irregular smoking can increase the risk of cancer. One study found that even people who smoked one to four cigarettes a day had much greater risks of dying from lung cancer or heart disease, while another found that even people who smoke just two cigarettes a day are more likely to develop cancers of the mouth and oesophagus (food pipe). And the EPIC study found that occasional smokers who have never smoked daily, still have higher risks of most cancers, and double the risk of bladder cancer.

Smoking is the only established preventable cause of pancreatic cancer, one of the most dangerous types of cancer in the UK

Starting smoking at an early age increases the risk of cancer even more. One study found that young smokers are especially vulnerable to DNA damage caused by chemicals in cigarette smoke. And when they quit, they have higher levels of DNA damage than people who started smoking later in life.

Smoking is a major cause of several types of cancer

Smoking also increases your risk of cancers of the bladder, cervix, kidney, larynx (voice box), pharynx (upper throat), nose, mouth, oesophagus (foodpipe), pancreas, stomach, liver and some types of leukaemia. And smokers are seven times more likely to die of these types of cancer than non-smokers.

There is some evidence that smoking could also cause other cancers including bowel cancer and Hodgkin's lymphoma.

⇨ Smoking is the most important preventable cause of bladder cancer and causes two in three cases in men and one in three cases in women. It increases the risk of this disease by three to five times.

⇨ Smoking doubles the risk of kidney cancer, and causes one in four cases in men, and one in ten cases in women.

⇨ Smoking is the number one cause of mouth and

oesophageal cancers, and together with alcohol, causes about nine in ten cases of these cancers. By the age of 75, a non-smoker has a one in 125 chance of developing these cancers, but a smoker's odds are one in 16.

⇨ Smoking is the only established preventable cause of pancreatic cancer, one of the most dangerous types of cancer in the UK. It causes over a quarter of pancreatic cancer cases.

⇨ Smoking is the most important preventable cause of stomach cancer and causes about one in five cases.

There is some evidence to suggest that smoking may increase the risk of breast cancer, bowel cancer and lymphomas but more research will be needed to say for sure.

Stopping smoking can reduce your risk

A large number of studies have shown that stopping smoking can greatly reduce the risk of smoking-related cancers. And the earlier you stop, the better. The last results from the Doctors' Study show that stopping smoking at 50 halved the excess risk of cancer overall, while stopping at 30 avoided almost all of it.

However, it's never too late to quit. One study found that even people who quit in their sixties can experience health benefits and gain valuable years of life.

The effects of stopping vary depending on the cancer. For example, ten years after stopping, a person's risk of lung cancer falls to about half that of a smoker. And the increased oral and laryngeal cancer risks practically disappear within ten years of stopping. But the risks of bladder cancer are still higher than normal 20 years after stopping.

Cutting down the number of cigarettes you smoke slightly reduces your risk of lung cancer, but you'll only experience the full health benefits if you stop altogether. One study found that even smokers who halved the number of cigarettes they smoked had similar risks of dying from heart disease and only slightly lower risks of dying from cancer.

Tobacco smoke contains many dangerous chemicals

Scientists have identified about 4,000 different chemicals in tobacco smoke. According to the International Agency for Research into Cancer and the European Network for Smoking Prevention, at least 80 of these chemicals could cause cancer. Many of the other thousands of chemicals are toxic and harmful to your health, including carbon monoxide, hydrogen cyanide and ammonia.

One study compared the amounts of cancer-causing chemicals in tobacco smoke with their ability to cause cancer. It concluded that the chemicals in smoke most likely to increase our risk of cancer include 1,3-butadiene, arsenic, benzene and cadmium.

Cigarettes contain at least 599 different additives including chocolate, vanilla, sugar, liquorice, herbs and spices. These are not toxic but they make cigarettes taste nicer and ensure that smokers want to continue smoking.

Tobacco smoke contains significant amounts of dangerous chemicals

Carbon monoxide is the fourth most common chemical in tobacco smoke and can make up 3–5% of its volume. Many of the other toxins are present in lower amounts, but some can still cause major damage at low concentrations.

Even single poisons can lead to substantial cancer risks. For example, benzene is a known cause of leukaemia. One study estimated that the benzene in cigarettes is responsible for between 10–50% of the leukaemia deaths caused by smoking.

Some studies have suggested that radioactive polonium-210 could account for much of the lung cancer risk caused by smoking. Polonium-210 becomes concentrated in hotspots in smokers' airways, subjecting them to very high doses of high-energy alpha-radiation. One study estimated that smoking 1.5 packs a day leads to as much radiation exposure as having 300 chest X-rays a year.

Chemicals in tobacco smoke can build up to harmful amounts

Many tobacco poisons disable the cleaning systems that our bodies use to remove toxins. Cadmium overwhelms cleaner enzymes that mop up toxins and convert them into more harmless forms. And many gases such as hydrogen cyanide and ammonia kill cilia, tiny hairs in our airways that help to clear away toxins.

So over time, tobacco poisons can build up to high levels in our blood, substantially increasing our risks of cancer and other diseases. By comparing the levels of toxins in smokers and non-smokers, some studies have found that smokers can have:

⇨ twice as much cadmium in their blood;

⇨ four times as much polonium-210 in their lungs;

⇨ ten times as much benzene in their breath;

⇨ ten times as much arsenic in their blood.

For most of us, much of our exposure to cancer-causing chemicals like benzene, formaldehyde, cadmium and nitrosamines comes from breathing in tobacco smoke. For example, one study found that smoking households have four times as much benzene in the air as non-smoking households.

The chemicals in smoke are more dangerous in combination than individually

The cocktail of chemicals in tobacco smoke is even more dangerous as a mix.

Chemicals such as nitrosamines, benzo(a)pyrene, benzene, acrolein, cadmium and polonium-210 can damage DNA. Studies have shown that benzo(a)pyrene damages a gene called p53 that normally protects our cells from cancer.

One study found that chromium makes PAHs stick more strongly to DNA, increasing the chances of serious DNA damage. Others have found that chemicals like arsenic, cadmium and nickel stop our cells from repairing DNA damage. This worsens the effects of chemicals like benzo(a)pyrene and makes it even more likely that damaged cells will eventually turn cancerous.

The poisons in cigarettes can affect almost every organ in the body

The many toxins in tobacco smoke can harm many different parts of your body.

Many tobacco poisons can damage your heart and its blood vessels. By comparing the amounts and strengths of different chemicals, one study found that hydrogen cyanide and arsenic alone can cause major damage to our bodies' blood network.

Acrolein, acetaldeyhyde and formaldehyde are most likely to cause diseases in our lungs and airways. Gases like hydrogen sulphide and pyridine can also irritate our airways, radioactive polonium-210 deposits damage surrounding cells, and nitrogen oxide constricts the airways, making breathing more difficult.

A protein called haemoglobin carries oxygen round our bloodstream. But carbon monoxide and nitrogen oxide stick more strongly to haemoglobin than oxygen, and reduces the levels of oxygen in our blood. This starves our organs of this vital gas.

Toluene can interfere with the development of brain cells. It also disrupts the insulating sheath that surround nerve cells, making them less efficient at carrying signals.

Nicotine is a very addictive drug

The Royal College of Physicians compared nicotine to other supposedly 'harder' drugs such as heroin and cocaine. They looked at many things including how these drugs cause addiction, how difficult it is to stop using them, and how many deaths they caused. The panel concluded that nicotine causes addiction in much the same way as heroin or cocaine and is just as addictive, if not more so, than these 'harder' drugs.

Smokers associate smoking with feeling good because nicotine makes the brain release dopamine – a chemical linked to feelings of pleasure. Smokers can also make mental links between abstract things like the taste of cigarettes or the feeling of smoking. These behaviours can become just as addictive as the nicotine itself.

Smokers are still exposed to dangerous chemicals if they smoke filtered or 'low-tar' cigarettes

Filters do not block out the many toxic gases in smoke, such as hydrogen cyanide, ammonia and carbon monoxide. They also do nothing to reduce levels of sidestream smoke from the burning end of the cigarette.

Some of the most dangerous chemicals in tobacco smoke, like hydrogen cyanide, are present as gases, and do not count as part of tar. This means that cigarettes with less tar are not necessarily any less dangerous.

Besides, researchers have found that people who smoked low-tar brands smoked harder and more frequently to satisfy their nicotine cravings. For example, in one study, low-tar smokers inhaled 40% more smoke per cigarette and ended up with similar nicotine levels as smokers who use normal brands.

And some smokers block filters with fingers or saliva. One Canadian study showed that over half of discarded cigarette butts showed blocked filters.

According to one study, low-tar smokers ended up inhaling about 80% more smoke, and had similar levels of cancer-causing chemicals in their blood. They can also inhale over twice as much tar and nicotine as smokers of normal brands.

Alcohol and other substances worsen the effect of smoking

Tobacco, as well as alcohol, can cause mouth, oesophageal and liver cancers. Scientists have also found that together, their effects are much worse. And while alcohol does not cause stomach cancer, it can worsen the risk of this disease in smokers.

One study found that together, smoking and drinking increased liver cancer risk by ten times. And a Spanish team found that people who smoke and drink heavily could increase their risk of oesophageal cancer by up to 50 times. This problem is made even worse because heavy drinkers and smokers often have poor diets.

Smoking also interacts with many other cancer risk factors and worsens their effects. For example, the lung cancer risk due to exposure to high levels of radon gas is 25 times higher in smokers than in non-smokers.

Second-hand smoking also causes cancer and kills thousands of people every year

Several studies have shown that breathing in other people's smoke causes cancer in non-smokers.

CANCER RESEARCH UK

Second-hand smoke contains several cancer-causing chemicals. Many of these chemicals are present in higher concentrations than in the smoke inhaled by the smoker themselves.

One study, which analysed 55 studies from around the world, found that non-smoking spouses of people who smoke at home have 27% higher risks of lung cancer. And a review of 22 studies found that people exposed to second-hand smoke in the workplace have 24% higher risks of lung cancer. Those who were exposed to the highest levels of second-hand smoke at work had twice the risks of lung cancer.

One study estimates that passive smoking may kill over 11,000 people every year in the UK from cancer, heart disease, strokes and other diseases.

Second-hand smoking also causes other health problems in non-smokers including asthma and heart disease. One study showed that even 30 minutes of exposure to second-hand smoke can reduce blood flow in a non-smoker's heart.

Children are especially at risk from second-hand smoking

Children are particularly at risk because they breathe faster than adults and have underdeveloped immune systems. A study by the Royal College of Physicians showed that about 17,000 children in the UK are admitted to hospital every year because of illnesses caused by second-hand smoke.

A large study of over 300,000 people found that children who were frequently exposed to cigarette smoke at home had a higher risks of lung cancer as adults. Another study found that children in households where both parents smoke have a 72% higher risk of respiratory diseases. And the EPIC study found that exposing children to second-hand smoke increases the risk of bladder cancer later on in life by a third.

Childhood exposure to second-hand smoke had also been linked to a wide range of other conditions including asthma, Sudden Infant Death Syndrome (or cot death), childhood meningitis and mental disabilities.

Smoking while pregnant can harm your baby

Smoking during pregnancy hinders the blood flow to the placenta, which reduces the amount of nutrients that reach the baby. Because of this, women who smoke while pregnant have lighter babies than those who don't smoke. And low birth weight can lead to higher risks of diseases and death in infancy and early childhood.

There is also evidence that women exposed to second-hand smoke during pregnancy also have lighter babies.

Smoking during pregnancy has also been linked to other pregnancy complications including miscarriage, stillbirth, ectopic pregnancy and cot death. It may also have consequences for the physical and mental development of the child.

Smokeless tobacco can also cause cancer

Smokeless tobacco, also known as chewing tobacco or snuff, is popular in South Asian communities in the UK. Many studies have shown that smokeless tobacco can cause oral cancer, and may cause pancreatic cancer. One study found that people who used smokeless tobacco had almost 50 times higher oral cancer risks than those who didn't.

The most dangerous chemicals in smokeless tobacco are called tobacco-specific nitrosamines (TSNAs). One review found that people who use smokeless tobacco expose themselves to up to a thousand times more TSNAs than non-smokers, and up to 50 times more than smokers.

Smokeless tobacco is also as addictive as cigarettes. Some studies found that the amount of nicotine absorbed from smokeless tobacco is three to four times greater than that delivered by a cigarette. The nicotine is also absorbed more slowly and stays in the bloodstream for a longer time.

A Swedish type of smokeless tobacco called snus is often promoted as 'safe' but studies have found that even this can increase the risk of oesophageal, stomach and pancreatic cancers.

⇨ Information from Cancer Research UK. Visit www. cancerresearchuk.org for more or to view references.

© Cancer Research UK

CANCER RESEARCH UK

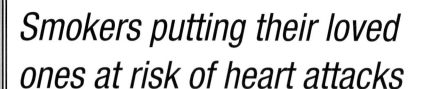

Smokers putting their loved ones at risk of heart attacks

Information from Addiction *journal.*

New research funded by the British Heart Foundation (BHF) and published today in *Addiction* journal shows that people living with someone who smokes continue to be at risk of the harmful effects of passive smoking.

Researchers at University College London and St George's, University of London measured recent exposure to tobacco smoke in non-smoking middle-aged men taking part in the British Regional Heart Study by measuring the levels of cotinine – a compound carried in the blood – at two time points 20 years apart. A blood cotinine level above 0.7ng/ml is associated with a 40% increase in the risk of a heart attack, and other studies have suggested that even a level of 0.2ng/mL may increase the risk. The researchers found that while in 1978–80, 73% of men had a cotinine level above 0.7ng/mL, by 1998–2000 that proportion had fallen to 17%.

However, despite the number of non-smoking men at risk having fallen, half of those who still had a high cotinine level (above 0.7ng/mL) in 1998–2000 lived with a partner who smoked. Non-smoking men who had a partner who smoked had average cotinine levels of 1.39ng/mL, almost twice the level associated with an increased risk of a heart attack. Their cotinine levels were nearly eight times higher than the cotinine levels of men whose partner did not smoke.

During the period the study looked at, national data shows that the prevalence of smoking amongst adults across the UK declined from 40% to 27% and the number of cigarettes consumed by smokers fell from 114 to 97 per week. Restrictions on smoking in public spaces and workplaces were also introduced, although the study period was before the national legislative bans on smoking in public places were introduced between 2006 and 2007.

Dr Barbara Jefferis from University College London, who led the research, said: 'The decline in smoking, together with restrictions on smoking in public places, has created an environment where people are exposed to far less tobacco smoke. This has resulted in the dramatic fall in the number of non-smokers at an increased risk of a heart attack.

'However, we can clearly see that living with someone who smokes puts you at a heightened risk. If we are going to reduce people's exposure to tobacco smoke

further then we will need to focus efforts on reducing smoking in the home.'

Professor Peter Weissberg, Medical Director at the BHF, said: 'This research shows that a great deal of progress has been made in reducing exposure to potentially damaging environmental tobacco smoke over the past 20 years. Importantly, it also shows that people are now more at risk of exposure in their own homes than in public places.

'We cannot stop people smoking in their own home, but we would urge smokers to think of the risk they're exposing their non-smoking friends and relatives to when they have a cigarette in the house.

'The BHF are calling for a proper plan to reduce the harm from smoking, including measures in the NHS Bill that will put an end to point of sale displays and prohibit cigarette vending machines, which are disproportionately used by underage smokers.'

10 February 2009

⇨ The above information is reprinted with kind permission from *Addiction* journal. Visit www.addictionjournal.org for more information.

© *Addiction*

ADDICTION JOURNAL

Under-18s guide to quitting

The younger you start smoking, the more damage there will be to your body when you get older. Here's seven reasons to quit and nine ways to help yourself do it.

Seven reasons to quit

1 You'll be healthier and less out of breath because smoking decreases your lung capacity.

2 You'll save yourself a packet. Smoking 20 a day for a year costs £1,825.

3 You'll look better. Chemicals in cigarettes restrict blood flow to your skin. Smokers have more wrinkled and saggy faces by the time they're in their mid-20s.

4 Quitting helps save the planet. Deforestation due to tobacco production accounts for nearly 5% of overall deforestation in the developing world, according to research published in medical journal the *BMJ*.

5 Someone who starts smoking at 15 is three times more likely to die from cancer than someone who starts smoking in their mid-20s.

> *Chemicals in cigarettes restrict blood flow to your skin. Smokers have more wrinkled and saggy faces by the time they're in their mid-20s*

6 The younger you start smoking, the more damage there will be to your body as an adult.

7 Not smoking will make you instantly more attractive. Most people prefer kissing non-smokers.

Nine ways to get through quitting

OK, enough of the arm twisting. You want to give up, so where do you start?

1 Make a deal with good friends to quit. You may find they want to as well.

2 It's very hard to give up using willpower alone, so get all the help you can find: 12- to 18-year-olds get free nicotine replacement therapy (patches, sprays, gum) on the NHS. Ask your GP. They won't be shocked you're a smoker.

3 Smokers often hate other people quitting, so be prepared for a few put-downs. It's a good idea to have something ready to say when you're offered a cigarette. Here are a few reasons (but we're sure you can think of better ones):

↳ 'Smoking costs me £xxx a year. I'm giving up so I can buy myself a new mobile/driving lessons/a holiday.'

↳ 'I can't smoke in my new weekend job so I want to give up.'

> *You'll save yourself a packet [by quitting]. Smoking 20 a day for a year costs £1,825*

Age started smoking regularly by sex, 2008. (Base: all who have ever smoked regularly: 2940 men and 2720 women [unweighted]).

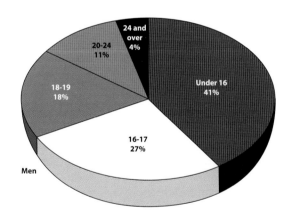

Men

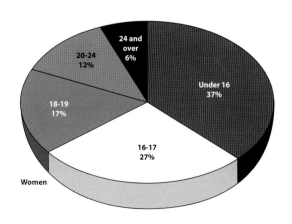

Women

Source: Smoking and drinking among adults, 2008, Office for National Statistics. Crown copyright 2010.

NHS CHOICES

'My boyfriend/girlfriend doesn't like kissing a smoker.' It's true: two-thirds of teenagers say smoking reduces sexual attractiveness.

'I'm taking my sport seriously and I need to give up if I want to be an athlete.'

4 Prepare for a tough few days when you first quit; the first days are the hardest to cope with for most people. But most of your withdrawal symptoms should have subsided after the first four weeks. Using nicotine gum and patches (Nicotine Replacement Therapy) is the best way to make coping with cravings more manageable.

5 Drink plenty of water to flush away the toxins in your system while you're quitting.

6 Worried about weight gain while you're quitting? Load your bag up with low-calorie snacks such as apple chips, carrot sticks, mints or chewing gum to get you through the cravings.

7 Get your family to support you. Your parents will be right with you on this. If they don't know you smoke, they might freak out at first, but if you tell them you're quitting they'll do all they can to help.

8 Do your best to stay away from alcohol, coffee, sugar and sweets while you quit. Studies have shown that these foods (especially the booze) can stimulate cigarette cravings.

Do your best to stay away from alcohol, coffee, sugar and sweets while you quit. Studies have shown that these foods (especially the booze) can stimulate cigarette cravings

---

9 And remember... it takes about a month for the nicotine cravings to subside. Take it one day at a time and soon you'll be smokefree for the rest of your life.

⇨ Reproduced from NHS Choices with permission. For more information, please visit the NHS Choices website at www.nhs.uk

Attitudes of young smokers

Young smokers think smoking is 'cool' but fear the future impact on their appearance.

Young smokers say concern about the effects of smoking on their appearance is a good reason to quit smoking, but not until they see visible changes to their appearance. This is the finding of a study by Professor Sarah Grogan of the University of Staffordshire and colleagues Gary Fry, Brendan Gough and Mark Conner, published today (26th January 2009) in the *British Journal of Health Psychology*.

87 smokers and non-smokers aged 17–24 took part in the study, based on focus groups. The smokers discussed how smoking impacted negatively on physical appearance (skin, teeth, hair and weight), and how they made sense of their smoking. The non-smokers also discussed a potential link between appearance and smoking, together with any appearance-related concerns that would discourage them from taking up the habit.

Male and female smokers were concerned about the impact of smoking on their appearance, but would quit only if skin ageing, wrinkling or other negative effects on appearance became noticeable. The young people did not consider themselves at immediate risk of such effects as they were thought to occur in older smokers only. Non-smokers expressed concern about the impact on skin and teeth if they started smoking.

Professor Grogan said: 'Young adults have the highest rates of smoking in the UK; they are also likely to be concerned with their physical appearance. Emphasising the fact that skin damage caused by smoking may not be visible to the naked eye – but is still happening – might be an effective way to motivate young people to quit.'

The findings of this study will be used to inform anti-smoking campaigns targeted at young people.

'Our study suggests that campaigns that emphasise the negative effects that smoking can have on appearance are more likely to encourage young people to quit than those that focus on the impact of smoking on health,' Sarah concluded.

26 January 2009

⇨ The above information originally appeared on the website of the British Psychological Society, www.bps.org.uk, and is reprinted with their kind permission.

NHS CHOICES / BRITISH PSYCHOLOGICAL SOCIETY

Up in smoke!

Information from Student UK.

OK, so you've heard the one(s) about how smoking causes emphysema, cancer and heart disease. And that it can irreversibly damage your lungs, heart, urinary tract, digestive tract, eyes, throat, bones, joints and skin.

But did you know that:

⇨ Legends Humphrey Bogart, Yul Brynner, Nat King Cole, Sammy Davis Jr, James Bond writer Ian Fleming, Betty Grable, Steve McQueen, Robert Mitchum, Frank Sinatra and Lana Turner (among many others) all died of smoking-related illnesses.

⇨ Smoking in women can contribute to infertility, early menopause, breast cancer and (eeek!) cancer of the vulva. Women who smoke and are on the Pill are also at risk for blood clots, strokes and heart attacks.

A recent report from the white coats reveals that women who smoke only three fags a day double their chance of heart attack. For men, it's between six and nine

⇨ Men who smoke are at risk of, among other horrible things, reduced blood circulation and atherosclerosis. Huh? Ruined blood vessels means male smokers won't be able to get a full erection and therefore, their bits will look quite a bit smaller.

⇨ Social smoking is also dodgy. A recent report from the white coats reveals that women who smoke only three fags a day double their chance of heart attack. For men, it's between six and nine.

⇨ Studies have shown that smokers seem to have less sex less often and less enjoyably, compared to non-smokers.

⇨ There are 43 elements contained in cigarettes that have been found to cause cancer. An average cigarette has such delightful ingredients as Acetone, Ammonia, Benzene, Cadmium, Carbon Monoxide, Formaldehyde, Hydrogen Cyanide, Lead, Mercury and Tar.

⇨ If you smoke 20 fags a day it will cost you £1,642.50 annually. Of which the government takes £1,292.18 in duty or VAT. You could spend that on about eight flights to Ibiza during the summer months.

Did ya? Bet you didn't.

Besides, it really doesn't look cool, it makes your teeth and breath go all manky, ensures that you will have to do twice as much laundry to get the stench out and it is an addiction. Even 'social' smokers have a habitual rather than clinical addiction.

So isn't it time you quit?

⇨ The above information is reprinted with kind permission from Student UK. Visit www.studentuk.com for more information.

© Student UK

STUDENT UK

How do I stop making excuses not to quit?

Quitting smoking isn't easy. The first step is deciding that you want to stop, and this means you have to stop making excuses to carry on smoking.

Common excuses – and the reasons you should ignore them – include:

Smoking helps me keep slim

Medical evidence shows that nicotine doesn't stop you getting hungry. Nicotine makes you burn calories faster, but as long as you remember that you need less food energy, quitting won't actually make you gain weight. Try eating low fat options and do an activity rather than replacing cigarettes with food.

Smoking calms me down

Actually, nicotine cravings between cigarettes make you feel stressed and anxious so when you have one you feel calm. You'll actually feel less stressed once you quit and don't have cravings. Wait for ten minutes and the craving will usually pass, and you'll feel better.

Try doing some deep breaths or take a walk, to distract you from cravings and relieve stress.

The damage to my health is already done

In fact, the evidence shows that the longer you smoke, the more at risk you become – so the sooner you quit, the healthier you'll be. As soon as you quit, your body starts to repair itself. You'll notice improvements to your breathing and senses of taste and smell just a few days after stopping smoking. You'll also improve the health of your family and friends by not exposing them to passive smoking.

It's not the right time to quit

Although it's true that you should try to avoid quitting during particularly stressful times, don't use this as an excuse to never get round to it. It's good to pick a particular date, such as No Smoking Day, the beginning of a holiday, or just the beginning of a working week. Work out what things make you want a cigarette, such as going to the pub, and try to pick a day when you can avoid this trigger.

My social life depends on smoking

You need to get your friends to support you in quitting; those who won't help you improve your health aren't really friends at all. Try to get a friend to quit at the same time, and avoid alcohol if you always smoke when you drink.

I can't quit, I'm addicted

To quit successfully you need to tackle both your chemical addiction to nicotine, and the fact that smoking has become part of your daily routine. The chemical addiction causes physical symptoms when you quit, such as tiredness, irritability, and difficulty concentrating. Your GP can prescribe medications to replace the nicotine, and counselling and support groups can give you added motivation to ignore your cravings. You should also try to change your routines, either replacing smoking with an alternative such as a drink of water or chewing gum, or doing something completely different such as cleaning, exercising, reading or taking up a new hobby.

⇨ Reproduced from NHS Choices with permission. For more information, please visit the NHS Choices website at www.nhs.uk

NHS CHOICES

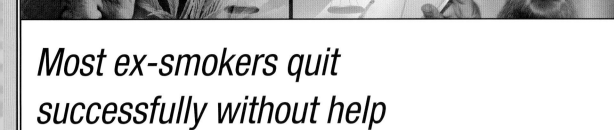

Most ex-smokers quit successfully without help

Information from Medical News Today.

Researchers reviewing hundreds of recent studies found that most ex-smokers ceased smoking successfully without help and found it less difficult than expected: they urge health authorities to do more to highlight this message and so that smokers' perceptions are not dominated by messages put out by tobacco control advocates and pharmaceutical companies who are overpromoting the idea that smokers need support like nicotine replacement products to help them quit.

The study was the work of Drs Simon Chapman and Ross MacKenzie from the School of Public Health at the University of Sydney, Australia and you can read a report about it in the 9 February issue of *PLoS Medicine*.

In their background information, Chapman and MacKenzie wrote that the dominant theme of messages about quitting smoking campaigns emphasise that if smokers are serious about quitting they should seek professional help or use nicotine replacement therapy. This has led to the 'medicalisation of smoking cessation', despite substantial evidence that most ex-smokers quit successfully either by going 'cold turkey', that is giving up all at once, or by reducing their consumption gradually and then giving up.

To arrive at this conclusion the researchers reviewed 511 studies published in 2007 and 2008. They found that the studies repeatedly showed that two-thirds to three-quarters of ex-smokers stop smoking without help, and most of them say that it was less difficult than they had expected.

The authors also found a dominance of pharmaceutical company-sponsored intervention studies, and cited a recent review of randomised controlled trials on nicotine replacement therapy that showed that 51 per cent of industry-funded trials reported significant cessation effects, while only 22 per cent of the non-industry-supported ones did.

They also found that many of the assisted cessation studies, but hardly any of the unassisted cessation studies, were done by researchers supported by a pharmaceutical company that made smoking cessation products.

The authors wrote that they believe there are three 'drivers' that force research on smoking cessation to concentrate on assisted cessation and neglect unassisted smoking cessation. These are what they describe as the 'dominance of interventionism', the 'increasing medicalisation and commodification of cessation', and the persistent yet erroneous tendency to quote the 'hardening hypothesis'.

By the 'hardening hypothesis', they mean the suggestion that where you have areas where not many people smoke, or where the most progress in quitting has been made, the smokers who remain are a 'hard core' that resists interventions, the idea being that those who have already quit were less dependent on nicotine and thus found it easier to give up, or they were more motivated to quit.

The authors said this hypothesis was so attractive that it caused the US National Cancer Institute to devote an entire monograph to it. Supporters of the hardening hypothesis argue that a greater proportion of today's smokers are 'hard core' and more addicted because the non-addicted ones have already joined the ranks of ex-smokers.

The authors said the hardening hypothesis has been heavily criticised, and quoted some evidence in support of this claim. For instance, data on smoking in the US for 2006–07 shows that in those states with low smoking prevalence, there has been a significant fall in the average number of cigarettes smoked daily, in the proportion of smokers who light up within 30 minutes of waking, and also in the proportion of those who smoke every day. This is 'compelling evidence against the hardening hypothesis', they wrote, because you would expect to see an opposite pattern if only hard core smokers were left.

They concluded that:

'Public sector communicators should be encouraged to redress the overwhelming dominance of assisted cessation in public awareness, so that some balance can be restored in smokers' minds regarding the contribution that assisted and unassisted smoking cessation approaches can make to helping them quit smoking.'

9 February 2010

⇨ The above information is reprinted with kind permission from Medical News Today. Visit www.medicalnewstoday.com for more information on this and other related topics.

© Medical News Today

Smoking 'worse for your health than being working class'

Smoking is worse for your health than being working class, according to a new study.

Scientists found that rich smokers were more likely to die young than non-smokers from the least affluent backgrounds.

Smoking also all but eradicated the traditional advantage in longevity that women enjoy over men.

'In essence, neither affluence nor being female offers a defence against the toxicity of tobacco,' said the researchers, who were led by Dr Laurence Gruer, director of public health science with NHS Health Scotland.

The findings come from a study involving more than 15,000 men and women in the towns of Paisley and Renfrew.

They were all middle-aged at the start of the research and were followed over the course of almost three decades.

Researchers found that a well-off professional who smoked was much more likely to die within the 28 years of the study than a non-smoking low-paid worker.

'In essence, neither affluence nor being female offers a defence against the toxicity of tobacco'

Fewer than one in four, 24 per cent, of well-off males who smoked throughout the study were alive by the end of it, compared to 36 per cent of less affluent non-smokers.

Just 41 per cent of rich females who smoked for the entire period of the study were still alive, the figures show, compared to 56 per cent of non-smoking working-class women.

Starting in the early 1970s the study followed 8,353 women and 7,049 men, all between the ages of 45 and 64 when the research began.

They divided the volunteers into 24 groups, based on their sex, social class and whether they were habitual smokers or not.

Smokers of all social classes were found to be at a higher risk of dying early than non-smokers from the

lowest classes, the study, published online in the *British Medical Journal*, found.

By the end of the study, 842 of the volunteers had died from lung cancer. Just five per cent of the deaths occurred among people who had never smoked.

Last year a report by the World Health Organization warned that babies born into some deprived parts of Britain would die 30 years younger than those in more affluent neighbourhoods.

On average, boys born in Britain can now expected to live to the age of 77, while girls can look forward to their eighties, predicted to die at an average age of 81.

But the Office for National Statistics also estimates a great variation based on social class, with boys in Kensington and Chelsea predicted to live to the age of 83, and those in Glasgow to just 71.

18 February 2009

THE TELEGRAPH

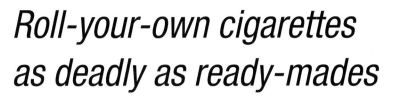

Roll-your-own cigarettes as deadly as ready-mades

Information from Cancer Research UK.

Roll-your-own (RYO) cigarettes expose smokers to similar levels of cancer-causing chemicals as manufactured cigarettes according to a new study by Cancer Research UK now published in *Addiction Biology*.

In the first study of its kind, researchers compared 127 urine samples of smokers who used ready-made cigarettes with 28 samples from RYO cigarette smokers to check the levels of two known cancer-causing chemicals.

There were no differences in the concentrations of the toxins between manufactured and RYO cigarette smokers even when age, sex, body mass index, puffing behaviour and nicotine exposure were taken into account.

Alarmingly, women had higher concentrations of these toxins irrespective of the cigarette type smoked.

> **There were no differences in the concentrations of the toxins between manufactured and roll-your-own cigarette smokers even when age, sex, body mass index, puffing behaviour and nicotine exposure were taken into account**

Lead researcher Dr Lion Shahab, from Cancer Research UK's Health Behaviour Research Centre based at UCL, said: 'Many smokers believe that RYO cigarettes are more "natural" and therefore are less harmful than manufactured cigarettes. The current findings suggest that this is not the case.

'These findings also show that women in particular accumulate higher concentrations of cancer-causing chemicals in their body whether they smoke RYO or manufactured cigarettes.'

Elspeth Lee, Cancer Research UK's head of tobacco control, said: 'These results further highlight that there's no such thing as a safe cigarette. Hand-rolled tobacco is more commonly used by people from lower socio-economic groups, and it is also in poorer communities

that smoking rates are highest. It's important that people know that using hand-rolled tobacco may be cheaper but is every bit as toxic as ready made cigarettes.

'Half of all long-term smokers will die from the addiction so it is important to continue working to reduce the impact that tobacco has on so many lives. Preventing children from starting smoking is vital. Putting tobacco out of sight in shops and getting rid of vending machines will all help to protect young people from the devastating influence of tobacco marketing. We're calling on Parliament to adopt these measures in the new Health Bill.'

7 July 2009

⇨ The above information is reprinted with kind permission from Cancer Research UK. Visit www.cancerresearchuk.org for more information.

© *Cancer Research UK*

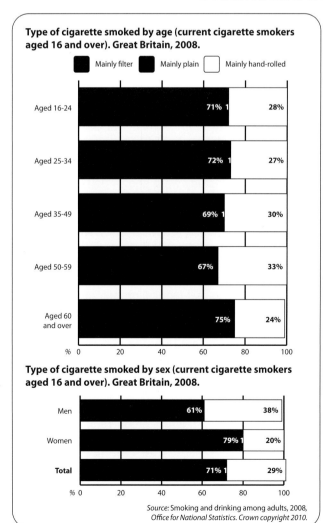

Type of cigarette smoked by age (current cigarette smokers aged 16 and over). Great Britain, 2008.

■ Mainly filter ■ Mainly plain ☐ Mainly hand-rolled

- Aged 16-24: 71% 1 / 28%
- Aged 25-34: 72% 1 / 27%
- Aged 35-49: 69% 1 / 30%
- Aged 50-59: 67% / 33%
- Aged 60 and over: 75% / 24%

Type of cigarette smoked by sex (current cigarette smokers aged 16 and over). Great Britain, 2008.

- Men: 61% / 38%
- Women: 79% 1 / 20%
- Total: 71% 1 / 29%

Source: Smoking and drinking among adults, 2008, Office for National Statistics. Crown copyright 2010.

CANCER RESEARCH UK

Cigarette pack design gives misleading smoke signals

Information from ASH.

New research from the University of Nottingham published today shows that tobacco branding and packaging send misleading 'smoke signals' to young people and to adult smokers. The research reveals that products bearing the word 'smooth' or using lighter coloured branding mislead people into thinking that these products are less harmful to their health. Since 2002 it has been illegal for manufacturers to use trademarks, text or any sign to suggest that one tobacco product is less harmful than another. But these regulations have clearly failed to stop misleading information appearing on tobacco packaging.

The research comes at a time of mounting pressure to strip packs of misleading branding, leaving only the name of the brand in a standard font. In Australia the Government's Preventative Health Task force has advised the Government to 'Eliminate promotion of tobacco products through design of packaging' as part of a comprehensive strategy to reduce tobacco deaths. In the UK, the Liberal Democrat front bench are to reintroduce an amendment to the Health Bill to introduce similar restrictions in the UK. The Health Bill is due to be debated on 12 October, the first day Parliament returns from its summer recess.

Participants in the study were shown pairs of cigarette packs and asked to compare them on five measures: taste, tar delivery, health risk, attractiveness, and either ease of quitting (adults) or which they would choose if trying smoking (children). Adults and children were significantly more likely to rate packs with the terms 'light', 'smooth', 'silver' and 'gold' as lower tar, lower health risk and either easier to quit (adults) or their choice of pack if trying smoking (children). For example, more than half of adults and youths reported that brands labelled as 'smooth' were less harmful than the 'regular' variety. The colour of packs was also associated with perceptions or risk and brand appeal. For example, compared to Marlboro packs with a red logo, cigarettes in packs with a gold logo were rated as a lower health risk by 53% and easier to quit by 31% of adults smokers.

The 516 adult smokers and 627 young people (aged 11 to 17) were also asked to rate plain packs where all branding was removed. Plain packs significantly reduced false beliefs about health risk and ease of quitting and were rated as less attractive and appealing by the children.

Lead author Professor David Hammond commented:

'A central feature of tobacco marketing strategy has been to promote the perception that some cigarettes are less hazardous than others, so that smokers worried about their health are encouraged to switch brands rather than quit. The truth is that all cigarettes are equally hazardous, regardless of what colour the pack is or what words appear on it. These tactics are giving consumers a false sense of reassurance that simply does not exist.'

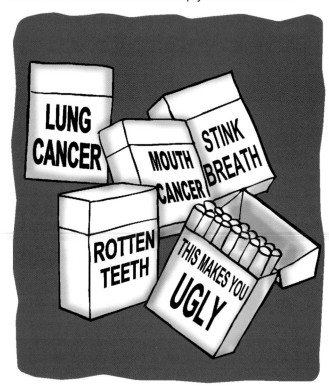

Deborah Arnott, Chief Executive of ASH, said:

'This research shows that the only sure way of putting an end to this misleading marketing is to require all tobacco products to be sold in plain packaging. That would remove false beliefs about different brands and communicate the message that all cigarettes are dangerous. This matter has been discussed by Parliament and there is now a perfect opportunity to include a requirement for plain packaging of tobacco products to be included in the Health Bill.'

4 September 2009

⇨ The above information is reprinted with kind permission from ASH. Visit www.ash.org.uk for more information.

© ASH

'More research' needed into safety of electronic cigarettes

Information from Cancer Research UK.

The need for more research into the long-term health effects of electronic cigarettes has been highlighted by scientists in the *British Medical Journal*.

Andreas Flouris and Dimitris Oikonomou, from the Institute of Human Performance and Rehabilitation in Greece, are concerned that not enough research has been carried out into the safety – or otherwise – of so-called 'e-cigarettes'.

Their position has been endorsed by Cancer Research UK, which is also concerned by the current lack of information.

Sales of the devices are thought to be increasing and a number of celebrities – including Kate Moss and Leonardo DiCaprio – have been spotted using them

E-cigarettes are battery-powered devices that simulate cigarettes by allowing the user to inhale a nicotine vapour.

Sales of the devices are thought to be increasing and a number of celebrities – including Kate Moss and Leonardo DiCaprio – have been spotted using them.

However, few studies have been conducted into the health effects of smoking e-cigarettes and those that have been published have reached differing conclusions.

One, carried out by the US Food and Drug Administration (FDA), found that the amount of nicotine provided with each puff often varies from the amount stated on the label, prompting the agency to express concern about e-cigarettes.

In contrast, a private enterprise called Health New Zealand (HNZ) found that the labelling on e-cigarettes reflected their actual nicotine content.

The FDA's research also detected the presence of diethylene glycol – a highly toxic liquid – in one of the cartridges it investigated, while both the FDA and HNZ found cancer-causing chemicals called tobacco-specific N-nitrosamines.

In its report, the FDA suggested that e-cigarettes may therefore be harmful, but HNZ recommended their use as they are likely to be less dangerous than tobacco products.

Meanwhile, a Greek organisation called Demokritos has maintained a neutral stance on the subject after conducting its own research.

Few studies have been conducted into the health effects of smoking e-cigarettes

Drs Flouris and Oikonomou note that this 'represents all the knowledge we currently have about e-cigarettes' and that the European Centre for Disease Prevention and Control is yet to publish any research on the subject.

'Alternative smoking strategies aimed at reducing the threat to public health caused by the tobacco epidemic are always welcome,' the researchers conceded.

However, they observed: 'To date, our knowledge about the acute and long-term effects of e-cigarette use is, at best, very limited.

'The scarce evidence indicates the existence of various toxic and carcinogenic compounds, albeit in possibly much smaller concentrations than in traditional cigarettes.'

Jean King, Cancer Research UK's director of tobacco control, said: 'There has been little research into how safe e-cigarettes are. And there's also very little regulation to control these products or their marketing. The only way to be sure of any risks or benefits is through rigorous testing.

'Anyone trying to quit smoking should use medicinal nicotine products such as patches, gum or inhalators, because these have been tested and found to be safe and effective. We believe that e-cigarettes should undergo the same rigorous tests and meet the same standards as all other medicinal products containing nicotine.'

21 January 2010

⇨ The above information is reprinted with kind permission from Cancer Research UK. Visit www.cancerresearchuk.org for more information.

© *Cancer Research UK*

CANCER RESEARCH UK

The economics of tobacco

Information from ASH.

Introduction

Smoking is a health problem, the costs of which include sickness, pain, grief and misery. It is impossible to value such impacts in monetary terms. However, smoking also plays a significant economic role in society. While cigarette tax is a significant source of revenue to the Treasury, the costs of smoking to the economy include not only the expense of treating diseases caused by smoking but also other costs such as working days lost and social security payments.

Cost to smokers

Currently, a 20-a-day smoker will spend about £2,000 a year on cigarettes. People on low incomes spend proportionally more of their income on tobacco than wealthier people. In 2008, households in the lowest income bracket spent £3.40 per week on cigarettes whilst those in the highest group spent £3.70 per week. This equates to 1.6 per cent and 0.4 per cent respectively of total weekly household expenditure.

The Treasury earned £8,219 million from tobacco duties in 2008–09

Smokers also pay with their health: the results from a 50-year study shows that half to two-thirds of all lifelong cigarette smokers will be eventually killed by their habit. Death is usually due to one of the three major diseases caused by smoking – lung cancer, chronic obstructive lung disease and coronary heart disease. Many who suffer from these diseases experience years of ill-health and subsequent loss of productivity. A Danish study concluded that smokers face a significantly higher chance of early retirement due to chronic disease.

Cost to the Government

Research commissioned by ASH has shown that the cost to the NHS of treating diseases caused by smoking is approximately £2.7 billion a year. Another study put the estimated cost as high as £5.2 billion. Other costs include the payment of sickness or invalidity benefits to those suffering from diseases caused by smoking and the payment of pensions and other family social security benefits to the dependants of those who die as a result of their smoking. However, it is also estimated that about £380 million a year is being saved by the NHS as a result of public health strategies such as the ban on tobacco advertising and the creation of the stop smoking services which have resulted in fewer people smoking.

In the 2008–09 financial year the Government spent £73.5 million on the stop smoking services in England plus an additional £56.2m on medicinal aids (e.g. nicotine replacement therapy). Expenditure on mass media health on smoking was £23.38 million.

An analysis of the cost benefits of achieving the Government's targets to reduce smoking has shown that £524 million could be saved as a result of a reduction in the number of heart attacks and strokes.

Fires

Cigarettes and other smoking materials are the primary cause of fatal accidental dwelling fires and have claimed the lives of 1,600 people in the UK over the past ten years. In 2007, smokers' materials accounted for 102 deaths – over a third of all accidental dwelling fire deaths. Since 1997, such deaths were becoming increasingly less common and there was a downward trend in the figures. In 2007, however, the number of these deaths rose for the first time in a decade. Smokers' materials are also responsible for the majority of non-fatal casualties in dwelling fires. In 2007, there were 1,047 casualties. The injury rate was highest for fires caused by cigarette lighters – 521 per 1,000 fires, a total of 251 injuries in 2007.

The costs of smoking to industry

Prior to the implementation of the law banning smoking in the workplace, smoking caused significant costs to industry. These included lost productivity caused by smoking breaks and increased absenteeism amongst smokers due to ill-health. It was estimated that each year about 34 million days were lost in England and Wales through sickness absence caused by smoking. In Scotland, the cost of this productivity loss was estimated to be £400 million per annum. Other costs to industry include cleaning and building maintenance costs. A review of the costs and benefits of making workplaces smokefree in England concluded that there would be a total net benefit of between £2.3 billion and £2.7 billion.

International studies

A study commissioned by the US tobacco company Philip Morris examined the economic impact of smoking on the Czech Republic. It concluded that tobacco smoking provided a net benefit to the economy, largely because of 'reduced healthcare costs' and 'savings on pensions and housing costs for the elderly' that would not have to be paid since smokers die earlier than non-smokers. In fact, the smoking costs were shown to be 13 times greater than the 'benefits'. A Danish study has shown that tobacco imposes a net cost to society even when taking life expectancy into consideration both in direct and indirect costs, while a study of the economic effects of a decline in smoking prevalence in New South Wales, Australia, found that the only sector that would be seriously affected would be the tobacco industry.

Tobacco taxation

The Treasury earned £8,219 million in revenue from tobacco duties in the financial year 2008–09 (excluding VAT). The UK has the highest tobacco taxes in the European Union. The price of a pack of 20 premium brand cigarettes currently costs around £6, of which £4.62 (77 per cent) is tax.

In July 1997, the Government announced its intention to raise cigarette taxes by at least five per cent above the rate of inflation each year, following the previous government's policy of raising tobacco duty by at least three per cent above inflation. This commitment was carried through in the 1998 and 1999 Budgets but in November 1999 the Chancellor abandoned this policy. Instead, he announced that any extra revenue raised from future tobacco tax rises would be spent on improved health care. From 2001 until 2008 tobacco taxes rose only in line with inflation. In 2009, tobacco duties were increased by two per cent on the basis of a deflationary forecast in the Retail Price Index of minus three per cent, thus representing a five per cent increase in real terms. In 2010, the Chancellor announced the tobacco duty would rise by one per cent above inflation for the current year and made a commitment to raising tobacco duty by two per cent above inflation from 2011 to 2014.

VAT on stop smoking aids

In the 2007 Budget, the Chancellor reduced the VAT on nicotine replacement products to the minimum level of five per cent, initially for one year. In 2008 this lower rate was extended indefinitely.

Tobacco smuggling

The price of tobacco is one of the most important factors affecting tobacco consumption. Increasing levels of tax on cigarettes reduces consumption because people respond to the price signal by giving up, cutting down or never starting. However, this policy can be undermined by the illegal importation of tobacco which is sold at reduced rates on the black market.

A study published in 2008 estimated that about 22 per cent of all tobacco smoked in the UK was smuggled – equivalent to 18 billion cigarettes out of a total market of 82 billion. As a result, the Government was losing more than £2 billion a year in revenue. However, the latest report from HM Revenue & Customs suggests that recently there has been a fall in smuggling with the illicit trade in cigarettes now accounting for about 12 per cent of the market (mid-point of range of estimates) while the illicit trade in hand-rolled tobacco is estimated to account for about 48 per cent of the total market. In 2008, the Government announced that the UK Border Agency and HM Revenue & Customs would work together on a new strategy to tackle smuggling.

The tobacco industry

British American Tobacco, the world's second largest tobacco company, is based in Britain, although the vast majority of its products are exported. In 2009, the company reported group operating profits of £4,101 million. The two principal UK tobacco companies – Imperial Tobacco and Gallaher (now owned by JTI) – control around 85 per cent of the UK market. In 2008, approximately 5,000 people were employed in tobacco manufacturing in Great Britain. According to tobacco industry estimates, in 1998 9,620 people were employed in tobacco manufacturing, accounting for 0.2 per cent of employment in all manufacturing activities in the UK.

Advertising and sponsorship

Since the implementation of the 2002 Tobacco Advertising and Promotion Act, tobacco advertising is now illegal except at the point of sale. Tobacco companies have exploited this loophole and since 2003 displays of tobacco products have become increasingly elaborate to stimulate sales, thus undermining the effectiveness of the law. Following a public consultation, the Government announced plans to ban the display of tobacco products at the point of sale. This was passed into law as part of the Health Act 2009 and will take effect from October 2011. In addition, sales of tobacco from vending machines will also be prohibited.

Studies have shown that tobacco advertising increases consumption and that advertising bans can lead to a drop in consumption of between five and nine per cent. The Government estimated that the tobacco advertising ban in the UK would lead to a drop in tobacco consumption of around three per cent, saving approximately 3,000 lives in the long term.

May 2010

⇨ The above information is reprinted with kind permission from ASH. Visit www.ash.org.uk for more information, and to view references for this piece.

© ASH

ASH

Forever cool: the influence of smoking imagery on young people

Information from the British Medical Association.

Why do young people smoke?

The way tobacco is perceived and how this integrates with self image is a crucial determinant of youth smoking. With the exception of tobacco marketing, these influences are often subtle and unintentional. The combination of circumstances prevails to create an environment in which both the prevalence and acceptability of smoking become exaggerated and eases the transition into the habit.

A mix of personal, social and environmental influences have been shown to encourage both the onset and continuance of youth smoking.

Personal

An individual's personal influences, including low self-esteem, lack of confidence and a heightened sense of vulnerability, can affect smoking attitudes and behaviour. These needs tend to be matched by a heightened belief in the benefits of smoking – that it can help in social situations, or is simply enjoyable. Regular smokers, for instance, are much more likely to feel that smoking can help you keep calm, compared with non-smokers. Young smokers and would-be smokers are also more likely to see tobacco as a means of expressing rebellion, reducing boredom and controlling weight. Young people, especially girls, have a desire to appear more mature and one way of projecting this image is to start smoking. Research with teenage girls in England found that they believed they were creating an 'adult social identity' and they valued being 'cool' and 'popular'. A strong association between anxiety and depressive symptoms and youth smoking has also been found, particularly in boys. With respect to the physical properties of tobacco, initial and continued smoking is related to underestimation of its addictiveness and health-damaging properties – and an overestimation of how easy it is to quit. Lack of success at school (both academically and behaviourally), and early leaving are also predictors of smoking. It is also associated with higher levels of alcohol and drug use.

Social

A young person's immediate social environment – especially the smoking behaviour and attitudes of significant others – has an important influence. Smoking by parents, siblings, and friends and peers are all important predictors of tobacco use. The ready availability of cigarettes both in the home and local community also predicts onset. Legislation preventing smoking in local communities can raise young people's perception of the social unacceptability of smoking.

The accessibility of tobacco products also forms an influential dimension of young people's social context. From studies conducted in the USA, a ready supply of cigarettes can be a stronger predictor of a young person's smoking behaviour than demand variables such as rebelliousness, psychopathology and peer smoking. In the UK, surveys conducted in 2006 found that two-thirds of regular smokers (individuals smoking at least one cigarette per week) aged between 12 and 15 years in England, and three-quarters of 15-year-olds and two-fifths of 13-year-olds in Scotland, reported buying their cigarettes from a tobacconist, newsagent or sweetshop. Just under a quarter of the 12- to 15-year-old current (regular and occasional) smokers in England reported that they found it difficult to buy cigarettes from a shop.

Environmental

Wider environmental factors are also an important consideration in determining smoking attitudes and behaviours. Social disadvantage can significantly impact on quit rates. Once started, young people from lower socio-economic backgrounds are much less likely to give up smoking than their wealthier peers. Media portrayals of smoking and the pervasive processes of tobacco marketing also form important additional parts of the wider environment. Both are known to have a great influence on youth smoking.

Smoking imagery

Young people typically encounter pro-smoking imagery from three sources: their social environment, the popular media and tobacco industry marketing.

Social environment

The immediate and wider environment is an important factor in promulgating positive images of smoking to young people. It is a pervasive and subtle phenomenon where much of the messaging comes from the fact that over a fifth of British adults still smoke, and in doing so, continue to reinforce the normalcy of the behaviour to

young people. Smoking by peers, siblings and friends brings the behaviour even closer to home, and can acquire particular prominence because it is so visible. In this way, young people's relationship with tobacco reflects that of society as a whole. This emphasises the need for comprehensive, population-level tobacco control policies.

Popular media

The popular media – films, television, magazines and more recently the Internet – form an extremely pervasive dimension of young people's social environment, and they frequently include references to tobacco. These references are not designed to promote smoking and any deliberate messaging is prohibited by UK legislation. Nonetheless, popular media may be having this effect and also generating pro-smoking imagery. As referenced in the sub-sections to follow, much research has been conducted into the extent of this messaging and imagery, and the influence it may be having on young people's smoking knowledge, attitudes and behaviour.

Films

Films have undergone the most extensive scrutiny, through a combination of content analysis, qualitative research and cross-sectional and longitudinal surveys, with most of the published research conducted in the USA. Images of smoking have been found to be commonplace in films, with frequency of portrayals decreasing between 1950 and 1990, but then increasing subsequently. A tendency for smoking to occur more commonly in youth-orientated rather than adult-targeted films has also been found since 2002 in the USA. Content analysis studies of internationally distributed films from the USA and India show that portrayals rarely identify the drawbacks of smoking – particularly the serious health consequences – and that the intensity of smoking has not reduced in line with prevalence rates. Nor does film smoking reflect the socio-economic reality of the habit, with smokers commonly portrayed as being rich and successful. These studies also show that smoking itself is frequently used to denote positive aspects of smoking, such as rebelliousness, relaxation and celebration.

The effects of film smoking on young people have been well documented. Qualitative studies show that young people are aware of smoking in films, feel that it is a realistic reflection of actual life and do not see it as influencing their own decisions. Findings from experimental studies, however, suggest that young people who are exposed to smoking in films tend to recall the references very accurately and take pro-smoking messages from it. These effects diminish significantly if the films are preceded by an anti-smoking commercial.

Cross-sectional studies in the US involving young people show a strong correlation between viewing films which include smoking, and pro-tobacco attitudes and behaviour. Among other effects, it is linked with overestimation of population prevalence rates among both smokers and non-smokers; a greater desire to smoke both now and in the future; more positive feelings about the habit among smokers; and more positive attitudes towards smoking among non-smokers. Conversely, on the rare occasions when smoking is portrayed in a consistently negative light these effects are reversed: a study with cinema-goers aged over 15 based around the tobacco industry whistle-blowing film *The Insider* showed a reduction in intentions to smoke.

Longitudinal surveys from the USA have also demonstrated a clear dose-response relationship between exposure to film smoking and increases in the likelihood of adolescents starting to smoke. A cohort study of over 3,500 10 to 14-year-olds, for example, found that 52 per cent of smoking onset could be attributed to smoking in the films. Other studies have also shown that adolescents who have a favourite film actor who smokes are more drawn to smoking, and that this effect was particularly strong among adolescent girls – although the direction of causation is unclear.

As noted, most of the research on smoking imagery in films has been conducted in the USA. Films from the USA, however, are widely viewed in the UK and elsewhere in the world. According to the UK Film Council, for example, 7- to 24-year-olds made up 45 per cent of cinema audiences of the top 20 films released in the UK in 2006. Of these, all 20 wholly or partly originated from the USA. The single published study on UK youth audiences used cross sectional analyses of data collected from 19-year-olds in Scotland from a longitudinal cohort surveyed previously as 11-year-olds. No association was found between the estimated number of occurrences of smoking seen in films and current or ever smoking at 19 years. In comparison, three recent studies examined the effect of films from the USA on youth audiences in Germany and Hong Kong. The findings from Germany and Hong Kong accord with the general trend from the research conducted in the USA described previously. The authors of the UK study concluded that more research should be conducted to determine whether the UK's discrepancy is due to age differences, cultural differences (including smoking prevalence) or methodological considerations.

Magazines

Research has found pro-smoking imagery to be commonplace in magazines. Content analysis demonstrates that smoking is portrayed in adverts, pro-tobacco editorial content and features. It is also found in incidental images (particularly following advertising bans) such as photo-shoots, fashion spreads, photos of celebrities and of everyday life, and images of events sponsored by tobacco companies.

A 1999 study in the UK of the top 12 youth magazines established that those magazines targeting young men had a significant amount of pro-tobacco advertising and editorial, whereas the women's magazines studied had none of the former and much less of the latter. Qualitative work with a sub-sample of these images shown to first-year higher education students (17- to 18-year-olds) revealed that the smoking imagery was attractive, sociable and reassuring, and reinforced respondents' smoker identities and perceptions of smoking. A study with individuals aged 12 to 13 and 15 to 16 found a strong relationship between smoking and images of smokers in fashion shoots taken from four style magazines. The younger age group were generally anti-smoking and interpreted the pictures on this basis. This age group showed less 'abstract' thought processes in interpreting the magazine images by describing their composition rather than what the images represented, as the older age group did. The 12- to 13-year-old age group was opposed to inclusion of the cigarettes in the fashion shots and found the smoking models' images intimidating, suggesting they looked 'tough'. The 15- to 16-year-old age group showed indifference and neutrality towards the presence of the cigarette in pictures, which can be interpreted as illustrating how 'ordinary' smoking is for this age group.

> **[Young people] identify with the social and stress-relieving aspects of smoking despite being aware of its harmful effects, and they perceive smoking in the media to be normal**

Much of the smoking imagery in magazines is not overtly pro-tobacco but studies show that it does have an impact on young people. They identify with the social and stress-relieving aspects of smoking despite being aware of its harmful effects, and they perceive smoking in the media to be normal. Thus smoking images in magazines act to reinforce the normalcy of smoking.

It should be noted that published research conducted in the UK on magazines and pro-smoking imagery predominantly comes from the previous decade and was conducted before the UK's tobacco advertising ban. The most recent post-ban evidence base is from international research, notably Australia. Carter et al (2007) argue that following the tobacco advertising ban in Australia, there was an increase in the prevalence of incidental smoking portrayals in Australian magazines. In their study, 14- to 17-year-old smokers and non-smokers were randomly assigned to a mock-up of a smoking or non-smoking youth magazine which they read before being interviewed using a structured questionnaire. 42 per cent of those who viewed the smoking magazine made unprompted mention of the smoking imagery. The imagery in the smoking magazine increased female non-smokers' intention to possibly take up smoking. This and an earlier UK study from 1998 found smokers view the general image of smoking more positively than non-smokers. Female smokers were attracted to male models who smoked while female non-smokers were repelled. Male smokers did not differ in response by magazine type.

Other media

Other forms of entertainment media have not been as extensively researched as films and magazines, but it is clear that smoking imagery is widespread. The Internet raises particular concerns in this respect due to the difficulty in regulating the content of websites. There is clear evidence that pro-smoking imagery is very extensive on the Internet, and is frequently linked to tobacco purchase opportunities, sex and excitement. This material, including social networking sites and user-generated video sites, is so pro-smoking that senior figures in tobacco control have suggested that the tobacco industry may be behind it. As highlighted in *Breaking the cycle of children's exposure to tobacco smoke* (BMA, 2007), it has been estimated that nearly all (98 per cent) young people aged 9 to 19 are Internet users, and nearly three-quarters (74 per cent) have online access at home, although this drops to around six in ten (61 per cent) for young people from a lower socio-economic background. The possibilities of using new media to reach this market are enormous. These include marketing techniques that are not covered under current legislation banning tobacco advertising. Viral marketing, for example, uses the Internet and mobile phone media to create 'word of mouth' awareness of marketing messages, commonly by encouraging consumers to pass on weblinks and downloads to their social networks.

Key message

The entertainment media are full of images that normalise smoking, making it appear both more common and acceptable than it really is. In this way it influences how young people perceive and attribute meaning to their own and others' smoking. It also reinforces the idea that cigarettes have social and cultural significance.

July 2008

⇨ The above information is an extract from information provided by the British Medical Association and is reprinted with permission. Visit www.bma.org.uk for more information or to view references for this piece.

© British Medical Association

BRITISH MEDICAL ASSOCIATION

Teenage smoking: it's my choice not yours

11-year study offers unique insight into why young people smoke.

Young people choose to smoke for their own personal desire and curiosity rather than because of the traditional concept of being forced into conforming with friends' behaviour, a new study highlights. Many adolescents stated they smoked as a stress reliever or simply because they liked it and wanted to, and not because of 'peer pressure'.

The new report, *The Liverpool Longitudinal Study on Smoking: Experiences, beliefs and behaviour of adolescents in Secondary School 2002-2006*, challenges current perceptions and offers a valuable insight into why young people smoke. Smoking within families was also a key influence, with many young people particularly highlighting that their parents smoked as a coping strategy. In turn, they were also likely to use this as a reason for their own smoking, reflecting the importance of the impact of family smoking habits.

The Liverpool Longitudinal Study on Smoking is an internationally unique research project undertaken by the Centre for Public Health at Liverpool John Moores University. Funded by the Roy Castle Lung Cancer Foundation, the research tracked 250 children from the ages of 5 to 16 to examine their experiences of smokers and smoking, and the factors that contribute to experimental smoking. This report is specifically looking at the responses of pupils aged 12 to 16.

Key findings show:

⇨ 99% of regular smokers lived with at least one smoker.

⇨ 14- to 16-year-olds living in deprived areas were 95% more likely to try smoking.

⇨ 82.6% of the group had been offered a cigarette.

⇨ 55% had tried a cigarette at some point during their school years.

⇨ 25% of smokers described themselves as regular smokers.

By the end of primary school less than 1% of pupils said that they wanted to smoke in the future; however, this study shows that by age 15, the number of smokers peaked at 55.6%. There was also a very significant increase in the number of smokers between the ages of 12 and 13, from 23% to 42%, which indicates that this is a crucial period in the onset of adolescent smoking, and one which should be targeted by smoking-prevention initiatives.

> **By the end of primary school less than 1% of pupils said that they wanted to smoke in the future; however, this study shows that by age 15, the number of smokers peaked at 55.6%**

The report forms part of an 11-year study in which researchers visited schools on an annual basis between 1995 and 2006, with pupils completing questionnaires, as well as taking part in interviews and focus groups.

Dr Susan Woods, who led the secondary school phase of the research, said that the aim of the study was to identify why young people smoke.

She said: 'The study was designed to explore young people's smoking uptake and practice and ground it in the social and cultural context in which they live. Without this we will never be able to fully understand the reasons behind adolescent smoking. By working with the young people the way we have, we have elicited vital information on their decision-making processes around smoking, their reasons for taking up the habit and the experiences that they draw on to make sense of smoking. Through this research we are able to better

CENTRE FOR PUBLIC HEALTH

understand the degree to which different risk factors predict smoking status, and how beliefs and attitudes towards smoking influence young people's actions.'

For some young people, smoking has been accepted into their daily lives for many years and focussing on changing influences around adolescents may lead them to make a different decision about smoking in the future. The role of parental smoking also cannot be under-estimated as this is a major influence in young people's smoking experimentation.

Dr Woods added: 'Tackling parental smoking may well be a successful indirect way of tackling adolescent smoking. In particular, initiatives to raise awareness amongst parents about the impact that household smoking rules have on uptake could be significant given the research found a clear relationship between living in a house with rules that advocate smoking and an adolescent trying smoking.'

14- to 16-year-olds living in deprived areas were 95% more likely to try smoking

The study highlights that young people feel strongly that they do, and should, have the power to make their own choice about smoking. Interventions that focus on the notion of being able to deal with 'peer pressure' may be misplaced, as the group already feel more than capable of dealing with friends or other people offering them cigarettes. The decision for adolescents is whether or not they want to try smoking, and make

their choice accordingly. The issue, more importantly is about exposure, and seeing so many other people all the time smoking around them and wanting to know what it is like.

'Tackling parental smoking may well be a successful indirect way of tackling adolescent smoking'

The Roy Castle Lung Cancer Foundation funded the unique research project. Chief executive Dr Rosemary Gillespie said: 'The process of becoming a smoker begins very early in childhood and is primarily influenced by exposure to smoke in the home.

'The findings provide us with a vital insight into how young people become smokers and will enable us to continue to develop and implement effective smoking prevention and health education programmes.'

Helping parents to stop smoking was the key to preventing their children from taking up cigarettes, she argued. 'The Government needs to apportion its efforts to support parents to stop smoking,' she said. 'The evidence shows that many people want to stop smoking but they need the support to do that.'

20 January 2008

⇨ The above information is reprinted with kind permission from the Centre for Public Health. Visit www. cph.org.uk for more information.

© *Centre for Public Health*

CENTRE FOR PUBLIC HEALTH

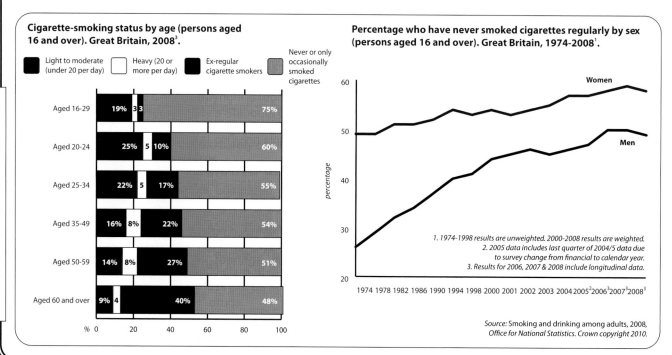

Cigarette-smoking status by age (persons aged 16 and over). Great Britain, 2008[3].

- Light to moderate (under 20 per day)
- Heavy (20 or more per day)
- Ex-regular cigarette smokers
- Never or only occasionally smoked cigarettes

	Light to moderate	Heavy	Ex-regular	Never or only
Aged 16-29	19%	3 3		75%
Aged 20-24	25%	5	10%	60%
Aged 25-34	22%	5	17%	55%
Aged 35-49	16%	8%	22%	54%
Aged 50-59	14%	8%	27%	51%
Aged 60 and over	9%	4	40%	48%

% 0   20   40   60   80   100

Percentage who have never smoked cigarettes regularly by sex (persons aged 16 and over). Great Britain, 1974-2008[1].

Women

Men

percentage

1. 1974-1998 results are unweighted. 2000-2008 results are weighted.
2. 2005 data includes last quarter of 2004/5 data due to survey change from financial to calendar year.
3. Results for 2006, 2007 & 2008 include longitudinal data.

1974 1978 1982 1986 1990 1994 1998 2000 2001 2002 2003 2004 2005[2] 2006[3] 2007[3] 2008[3]

Source: Smoking and drinking among adults, 2008, Office for National Statistics. Crown copyright 2010.

ISSUES: TOBACCO AND HEALTH   **28**   chapter two: smoking and society

Cigarette pack health warnings 'could encourage people to keep smoking'

Cigarette packets with serious health warnings could actually encourage people to continue smoking, research suggests.

According to a study, smokers who are continually confronted with warnings that cigarettes kill actually develop coping mechanisms to justify continuing their habit.

Comparatively, if smokers are shown warnings suggesting the habit could make them unattractive, they are more likely to give up. Teenagers who took up the habit to impress or fit in with their peers were more likely to be influenced by warnings about their appearance, the study found.

'In general, when smokers are faced with death-related anti-smoking messages on cigarette packs, they produce active coping attempts as reflected in their willingness to continue the risky smoking behaviour,' the study said.

'To succeed with anti-smoking messages on cigarette packs one has to take into account that considering their death may make people smoke.'

The study from the United States, Switzerland and Germany, led by Jochim Hansen of New York University and the University of Basel, asked 39 psychology students who said they were smokers, aged between 17 and 41.

Participants filled in a questionnaire determining how much their smoking was based on self-esteem, before being shown cigarette packets with different warnings on them. Half of them read warnings such as 'Smoking leads to deadly lung cancer', while the other half had warnings about attractiveness.

After a 15-minute delay the students were asked more questions about their smoking behaviour and if they intended to quit.

The study, published in the *Journal of Experimental Social Psychology*, found that cigarette packets with death-related warnings were not effective and even caused more positive smoking attitudes.

'On the other hand, warning messages that were unrelated to death effectively reduced smoking attitudes the more recipients based their self-esteem on smoking.

'This finding can be explained by the fact that warnings such as "Smoking brings you and the people around you

severe damage" and "Smoking makes you unattractive" may be particularly threatening to people who believe the opposite, namely that smoking allows them to feel valued by others or to boost their positive self-image.'

A Department of Health spokesman said: 'Health warnings on tobacco packaging have played an important role in helping smokers understand the risks of tobacco use and where to get help to quit. Research from around the world has shown that different people react to different types of messages to motivate them to attempt to quit.

'In October 2008, the UK was the first nation in the European Union to introduce graphic picture warnings to cigarette packets that showed smokers the grim reality of the effects smoking can have on their health. We are now currently working with the European Commission to develop new pictorial warnings for tobacco packaging, including testing different types of messages with smokers.'

9 December 2009

THE TELEGRAPH

Social stigma prevents pregnant smokers seeking help to quit

⇨ **One in four (28%) pregnant smokers would like to seek help to stop smoking but are worried about being judged[1].**

⇨ **Powerful new campaign shows that every cigarette smoked restricts the essential oxygen supply to an unborn baby, so that their tiny heart has to beat harder every time a pregnant woman smokes.**

⇨ **Half of people (49%) are critical of pregnant women who smoke.**

⇨ **New NHS Smokefree pregnancy campaign calls for 'encouragement not judgement' for pregnant smokers.**

The NHS Smokefree team has launched a powerful new campaign to raise awareness of the dangers of smoking, and the immediate benefits of becoming smokefree, for pregnant women and their babies. The campaign, supported by Dr Miriam Stoppard, seeks to encourage public support for pregnant women in their quit attempts and to drive take-up of the specialist pregnancy NHS Stop Smoking Services available to help them.

As the baby shares the mother's bloodstream, the womb does not protect the unborn baby from cigarette smoke

The new campaign will target the 100,000 (17%) of pregnant women in England who smoke during their pregnancy by communicating why smoking is harmful to them and their baby. The campaign will lead on the fact that every cigarette smoked restricts the essential oxygen supply to an unborn baby, so that their tiny heart has to beat harder every time a pregnant woman smokes. The campaign reinforces the message that every cigarette harms the unborn baby, and that stopping smoking – no matter how far along the pregnancy is – will benefit the woman and her baby immediately.

New research from the NHS Stop Smoking Service[2] reveals how the social stigma around smoking during pregnancy can have a negative impact on the willingness of pregnant smokers to seek help, with over a quarter of pregnant smokers (28%) admitting they would like to seek support to stop smoking but are worried about being judged. A further third of pregnant smokers say

they sometimes hide their smoking as they are worried about people criticising them (38%) and a third (39%) admit that they are ashamed to admit that they smoke to their midwife or healthcare professional.

Dr Miriam Stoppard, who specialises in women's health, said: 'Pregnant women who smoke do not automatically find it easy to stop smoking as soon as they become pregnant, often hiding their smoking rather than asking for help to quit, because they feel that they will be criticised.

'Pregnancy can be a particularly difficult time to stop smoking – and rather than stigmatising these women, we should be guiding them to their local NHS Stop Smoking Service for expert advice and support to help them quit.'

Polling from YouGov[3] on behalf of the NHS Stop Smoking Service highlights the need for greater public empathy for the struggles that many pregnant smokers face, with only 1% of people considering pregnancy to be the most difficult time to stop smoking. In addition, over half (55%) of people think that women who smoke when they are pregnant are not taking the responsibility of motherhood seriously, and 49% are critical of pregnant smokers.

Unsurprisingly however, it is other mothers who are most understanding about pregnant smokers, with a Mumsnet poll revealing that 84% of mothers[4] think that women who smoke during pregnancy need help and support to quit rather than public condemnation.

To respond to the specialist needs of women who smoke during pregnancy, there is dedicated NHS support to help pregnant women to quit. The NHS Pregnancy Smoking Helpline – 0800 169 9 169 – offers a free and friendly service that provides practical advice about stopping smoking. Pregnant women can sign-up to receive regular phone calls which provide flexible ongoing support and

SMOKEFREE NHS

encouragement. In addition, there are over 150 local NHS Stop Smoking Services throughout the country, offering a range of services and the majority offer pregnancy specific support services.

Research has shown that smokers who quit with NHS support are up to four times more likely to succeed.

Ex-smoker Chantelle Hankin from Strood in Kent, who is six months pregnant with her third child, comments: 'People do judge women who smoke while they're pregnant, which made me initially concerned about admitting I needed help. When I approached my local NHS Stop Smoking Service however, they were incredibly helpful and encouraging. They recommended the regular group support sessions, which I really enjoyed attending every week and which motivated me to succeed. I've been smokefree for over two months now and haven't looked back.'

Lisa Fendall, Midwife NHS Specialist Smoking in Pregnancy Adviser for Rotherham said: 'We see lots of pregnant women who are worried about trying to stop smoking and feel they don't have the support or anyone to talk to about it. We're making sure they see there is plenty of help on offer, from pregnancy focused one-to-one or group support sessions at their local NHS Stop Smoking Service or the NHS Pregnancy Smoking Helpline giving friendly advice and support – we work together to find the best solution for them.'

As part of the new campaign, midwives have been provided with new tools and information to support their work in helping pregnant smokers stop smoking. These include a new leaflet and a Smoking in Pregnancy Support DVD.

Quitting is not easy and it can take some smokers several times to get off cigarettes for good.

Smoking in pregnancy fast facts/key messages

Stopping smoking during pregnancy is the single most important step a mother can take to benefit her health and her baby's health.

As the baby shares the mother's bloodstream, the womb does not protect the unborn baby from cigarette smoke. Cigarettes contain over 4,000 chemicals, including carbon monoxide, nicotine and cyanide, all of which are passed onto the baby every time the mother smokes.

As babies need oxygen to grow, their development can be affected. Smoking is the main cause of low birth weight in babies.

Smoking while pregnant is far more damaging to the baby's health than any stress that comes from quitting.

It's never too late to stop smoking. Once the mother stops smoking the baby will benefit immediately and the oxygen supply will quickly return to normal.

It is important for the partners of pregnant women to try to quit smoking too because if the partner smokes, the pregnant smoker will find it much more difficult to quit successfully. In addition, regular exposure to secondhand smoke results in low birth weight.

Smokers are up to four times more likely to stop smoking successfully if they use the NHS Stop Smoking Services and nicotine replacement products. Some nicotine replacement therapies (NRT) are now licensed for use during pregnancy. GPs, specialist stop smoking advisers, midwives, healthcare visitors and pharmacists can offer appropriate advice.

NHS Support available

The NHS Pregnancy Smoking Helpline (0800 169 9 169) operates from 12pm to 9pm daily, and offers a free and friendly service that offers practical advice about stopping smoking.

The helpline will also send pregnant women information leaflets and details of their nearest local NHS Stop Smoking Service.

There are over 150 local NHS Stop Smoking Services throughout the country, offering a range of services and the majority offer pregnancy specific support services.

Local NHS Stop Smoking Services may offer one-to-one home visits, one-to-one or group support sessions with trained stop smoking advisers.

Pregnant women can also sign-up to receive regular phone calls from the NHS Pregnancy Helpline, which provide flexible ongoing support and encouragement.

To find a local NHS Stop Smoking Service call the NHS Pregnancy Smoking Helpline on 0800 169 9 169 or visit www.nhs.uk/smokefree

The NHS Smoking in Pregnancy campaign has produced a free Smoking in Pregnancy Support DVD. This is encouraging and supportive and includes case studies of pregnant women who have stopped smoking and information about all of the NHS support options. Pregnant women can get the Smoking in Pregnancy Support DVD through their midwife or by calling the NHS Pregnancy Smoking Helpline (0800 169 9 169).

Top tips for pregnant women going smokefree

Chuck out your ashtrays, matches and lighters and anything else you needed to smoke. Put potpourri where your ashtrays used to be – your home will smell fresher in no time at all.

Start a savings jar today. Put all the money you're saving by not smoking in a clear jar every day and watch how fast it grows.

Tell everyone that your home is a smokefree zone so you won't be tempted by people smoking in front of you and your baby won't be suffering from other people's smoke.

Work out when and where you used to smoke so you know when your trigger times are, and think of ways to avoid them. Try sitting somewhere else when you drink your tea or getting up after dinner to go and put some hand cream on.

If you're really finding it tough, there are some nicotine replacement therapies that are safe to use in pregnancy and they're free on prescription for pregnant women. They can really help you beat the cravings. Just ask your stop smoking adviser, GP, midwife, health visitor or pharmacist.

Quitting smoking can be stressful. Chill out by taking a soak in the bath whenever you can.

Get as many scan pictures as you can and put them up around the house, especially in those places you used to smoke. Every smokefree day makes a difference to you and your baby.

If cigarettes tempt you back, the special NHS Pregnancy Smoking Helpline can help you get back on track. Their specialist advisers really do understand what you're going through and are there to help. Go on, give them a call on 0800 169 9 169.

Try going swimming. It's great exercise for pregnant women because the water will help to support your bump.

Cravings are hard, but they only last a few minutes. Try writing down ten possible baby names for a boy and a girl. Craving still bad? Make a list of the worst baby names you've ever heard.

Notes

1 Research undertaken by Continental Research on behalf of the Department of Health. Figures reported are based on partial survey data only. Sample size was 224 pregnant women, aged 16+, who currently smoke (England only). Fieldwork was undertaken between 12–27 January 2009 (with fieldwork continuing until 01/02/09). The survey was carried out face to face, in-street.

2 As above.

3 All figures, unless otherwise stated, are from YouGov Plc. Total sample size was 2136 adults. Fieldwork was undertaken between 16–19 January 2009. The survey was carried out online. The figures have been weighted and are representative of all GB adults (aged 18+).

4 Mumsnet online poll of 1079 mothers, conducted between 15–21 January 2009.

5 February 2009

⇨ The above information is reprinted with kind permission from Smokefree NHS. Visit http://smokefree.nhs.uk for more information.

© Crown Copyright 2010 - nhs.uk

Proportion of smokers who would like to give up smoking altogether, by number of cigarettes smoked a day. Current cigarette smokers aged 16 and over, Great Britain, 2008.

Men
0-9 59%
20 or more 62%
10-19 65%

Women
0-9 69%
20 or more 64%
10-19 66%

Source: Smoking and drinking among adults, 2008, Office for National Statistics. Crown copyright 2010.

War on smokers: the backlash

The Government wants to halve the number of cigarette users,
infuriating the tobacco industry and die-hard smokers.

This week, the Department of Health put out a 70-page document titled *A Smokefree Future*, full of plans to make cigarettes the preserve of a very hard-bitten minority. On the front, a twentysomething father looks lovingly at his young son. Inside, scores of other parents are doing the same – all apparently enjoying the health and happiness that comes from a life without cigarettes.

Having banned smoking in all enclosed public spaces in 2000*, thereby securing a 25% drop in recorded numbers of smokers, the Government's new aim is to cut the proportion of us who smoke by another half – so that by 2020, only one in ten Britons will still have the habit.

The proposed means to such an ambitious end include a new 'doorway ban' on those droves of sad smokers who cluster in the entrances of workplaces, the expanded issuing of nicotine patches, the selling of cigarettes in plain packaging, the removal of tobacco products from display in shops, the banning of vending machines – and, just in case any top-flight athletes are hoping for a few pre-race gaspers – 'a tobacco-free London 2012 Olympics'.

In Scotland, things are a little further along: late last month, the Edinburgh parliament passed new legislation for much the same measures. So it is that the UK is moving yet further into the post-cigarette age: something that, for those of us who are old enough to remember a smoke-fugged country where the habit was all but encouraged, may prompt either a shiver of nostalgia, a sharp feeling of relief, or an ambivalent mixture of both.

If you are in your mid-40s or over, you will probably recall cigarette adverts on TV, mass smoking on public transport (the London Underground was a particular joy), the pleasures of motoring trips with perma-smoking adults, celebration boxes of fags that were obligatory for any family Christmas (we had JPS ones in our house, packaged in a huge black tube), and much more besides. Chatshow hosts and guests puffed freely, footballers had a crafty cig at half-time, and even high-profile athletes were partial. If you doubt this, you should Google a hurdler named Shirley Strong, Olympic silver medallist and unabashed smoker, and marvel at what a weird place the world once was.

But no more. Smoking may still be on the rise in developing countries, by around 3.5% a year, but in most of the industrialised world, it's all falling numbers, anti-smoking zeal, and grim Government statistics. You probably know the relevant figures: according to the official numbers, smoking causes 80,000 deaths in England each year, and costs the NHS an annual £2.7bn – and on a worldwide scale, cigarettes kill more people than illegal drugs, road accidents, diabetes and alcohol abuse put together. In the last century, smoking is estimated to have taken the lives of around 100 million people.

Still, in this country, around ten million of us still do it. Behind that figure lurks no end of sociological intrigue. In our prisons, 70% of inmates smoke. Age-wise, smoking peaks in the 25–34 age group at 26%, and falls to its lowest among the over-60s. Among men of Bangladeshi origin, more than 40% are tobacco-users; but women from the same background hardly bother at all, registering a figure of 2%.

Yorkshire has the greatest regional concentration of smokers, at 25% of the population; London and the east of England bring up the rear at 19% each. As for pregnant women, 14% continue to smoke, and that figure is based on people filling in their own forms, so it's safe to assume it's actually higher.

By far the most clear-cut differences surround how smoking rates reflect the lifestyles of the UK's social classes. Among young illicit smokers, take-up rates across income and wealth divides are reasonably similar, but once adulthood kicks in, the better-off tend to quit, while those lower down the social scale are much more likely to carry on. The fifth of the population with the highest incomes register a smoking rate of 15%, whereas in the lowest income group, the figure is nearly twice that – and though smoking rates over the last decade have come down among the population as a whole, those classed as 'manual workers' have only managed a paltry drop of two percentage points, from 31% to 29%.

And now, as smokers shiver outside pubs, clubs and factories, the Government is coming for them – though this time, using rhetoric more cautious and cuddly than the stereotype of some great anti-smoking clampdown might suggest.

When I catch health secretary Andy Burnham on his way to yesterday's cabinet meeting, he is full of talk about 'going with the grain of human behaviour', avoiding the invasion of people's private space, and assuring smokers that if they want to carry on blitzing their lungs and arteries and pouring money into the pockets of both the tobacco companies and the Treasury, it's their choice – though help is available, and more accessible than ever. The essential point, he claims, is to go for policy that's

'heavily targeted on the new flow of smokers coming in, rather than restricting the liberties of smokers who are already there. If they look at where I was focusing my efforts yesterday, I hope they'll see that.'

'At times,' he tells me, 'we've allowed ourselves to have this "nanny state" tag thrown at us, by not being clear about the limits of where it's right to go. We've got to be more cautious and precise in our language.' He is, he tells me, instinctively opposed to outlawing smoking in cars (even with children on board). But, like a good New Labourite, neither is he opposed to 'having a debate'.

When I ask him about the so-called 'doorway ban', by contrast he sounds altogether more certain. 'A doorway is part of a building, essentially,' he says. 'So where people are coming through, and there's lots of smoke around the entrance, and it gets wafted into the building – well, that's not an ideal situation, and it's not consistent with the ban.'

As for pregnant women, 14% continue to smoke, and that figure is based on people filling in their own forms, so it's safe to assume it's actually higher

---

As ministers and politicians continue their ongoing anti-smoking drive, a battle akin to the later stages of the cold war grinds on, with a besieged British tobacco industry in the role of the Soviet Union, facing off against the strident anti-tobacco lobby. Every time the Government moves on smokers, the industry issues the usual protests about freedom of choice and human beings' inalienable rights to basic pleasures, often joined by a small handful of militant smokers who see the Government's attempts to wipe out their habit as the stuff of outrageous authoritarianism.

Over Christmas, David Hockney used his guest editorship of Radio 4's *Today* programme to inveigh yet again against the evils perpetrated by anti-smokers – and when he calls me from his home in Bridlington, he needs no encouragement to do so yet again. A somewhat chaotic ten-minute diatribe includes – rather rumly – the recent death of the Labour MP David Taylor, who played a key role in pushing the smoking ban through Parliament. 'I noticed that on Boxing Day, he went for a walk, and dropped dead aged 63,' he says. 'If I'd have dropped dead, they'd have said it was my lifestyle. Nobody mentioned his meanness of heart.'

Somewhat predictably, he disagrees with Burnham's insistence that, with these new measures, the Government is not trying to restrict smokers' freedom. 'It has gone much, much too far,' he says. 'I'm really outraged now.' He traces his ire to 'this f*****g little mean-spirited country: I see Martin Amis says it's third-rate, but it's tenth-rate

now.' He ends with: 'There's an awful lot of smokers who live to ripe old ages. Now, why is that? Why? Obviously, genes trump everything. Some people shouldn't smoke, but some people are perfectly happy smoking. Picasso, Monet, Matisse – they all smoked, and they all lived to ripe old ages, with very generous lives. Didn't they? Yes, they did.'

Beyond voices like his, there is a whole tangle of blogs, websites and pressure groups (including the pub lobby, who chiefly blame the smoking ban for Britain's current epidemic of closures), and, of course, the massed power of the tobacco industry.

Christopher Ogden is the 56-year-old chief executive of the Tobacco Manufacturers Association: a former army major who says he was drawn to speaking up for the tobacco industry by a lifelong belief in 'freedom of choice and freedom of speech and fair play'. Needless to say, he is a smoker himself.

'Enough is enough,' he tells me. 'The Government have introduced such a huge range of tobacco control measures that it's almost as if they're running out of ideas. We've had the ban on advertising and promotion, the raising of the age of sale from 16 to 18, the smoking ban, the graphic pictorial health warnings. Now we've got vending and display bans. What more do they want to do?'

The one chance of a reprieve, he suggests, lies in slightly more sceptical noises coming from the Tories: he would presumably be cheered by an off-the-record Tory spokesperson telling me that many of the Burnham plans are 'pretty unenforceable' and 'not evidence-based', though there again, the same source is at pains to tell me that his party 'supports any action that will reduce smoking'.

Speaking to advocates for the tobacco industry is always a grimly amusing business, as you listen to people somehow acknowledging that smoking is not exactly good for you, while trying to wriggle free of specifics. When I ask Ogden about smoking's links to lung cancer, he says: 'It's not in my gift to say. I wouldn't want to attribute it to any particular illness. I'd just say the consensus is that there are health risks associated with it.'

My mention of heart disease is similarly dodged. Even the connections between parental smoking and Sudden Infant Death Syndrome (or cot death) get short shrift. 'I don't have a position on that. I'm not privy enough to the science to give a comment.'

But aren't the numbers of British smokers in inevitable decline? 'Who knows?' he says. 'I mean, fashions change, don't they? Society changes. Could smoking come back? I can't predict the future, but it's certainly a possibility, yes. Why not?'

How many a day does he smoke? 'About a packet.' And does he have moments of concern about his health? 'Not at all.' So does he think he'll smoke till he dies? 'Oh, no.

I shall probably give up at some point, as I have in the past. I've been through phases of my life where I haven't smoked for five years at a stretch. And I've decided to go back to it.'

Why give up? Why not just carry on puffing away on his industry's output until he croaks? 'Well, we're all going to go one day.'

Over at Ash – Action On Smoking and Health – Ogden's opposite number is Deborah Arnott. She was fond of the occasional cigarette until 2003, when she decided to leave a job in TV production and devote her working life to the anti-smoking struggle. 'I smoked Silk Cut,' she says, 'which probably shows my age.'

Though she's in favour of going further than the Government (she supports a complete ban on smoking in cars, whether they contain children or not), she says the new strategy deserves plenty of applause, chiefly because moves against smoking must be regularly renewed and extended, as proved by evidence from abroad. To pause is to run the risk of the numbers once again increasing: in Ireland, she tells me, the Government successfully brought in smoke-free legislation, but 'they didn't do anything else, and smoking started to creep back up again'. Much the same thing apparently happened in Finland, where a similar failure to keep up the anti-smoking momentum meant that cigarette use stayed at much the same level and, among women, went up.

'There's a theory about this,' she says, 'which is that there's always an upward pressure on smoking. That's because it's still something that's attractive to young people, because it's still cool. If you talk to eight-, nine- or ten-year-olds, they'll be very anti-smoking. Puberty is when it happens: you're independent, you want to be cool, and you're not sure what do with your hands when you're talking to people of the opposite sex.'

But how do you fight that? You can't ban pictures of Kate Moss smoking at awards ceremonies. 'No, you can't. And that's difficult. But over generations, that will change. You need it to stop being seen as cool. And it's beginning to go that way. My children went to a comprehensive in central London – and actually, what amazed me was that they used to come home at night, and they didn't smell of smoke. It is becoming less cool.'

Back in Westminster, Burnham suggests that in the early-to-mid 1980s, he was ahead of the generational curve. His experience of smoking, he assures me, is very limited indeed – because even as an impressionable youth, he found the supposed attractions of cigarettes baffling. 'I had a couple under the slide in a park when I was 14, and that was it,' he says. 'I couldn't cope with it. I genuinely have never seen any upside from it. I think it's a unique activity in that sense.'

Does he foresee a time when, in Britain at least, nobody smokes at all?

What he says next would surely chill your Hockneys and Ogdens to the marrow. 'Honestly? I can imagine a day when people say, "Why did it happen?" The costs, the health effects, what it does to your appearance, the smell... I can imagine people saying, 'Why did we ever do that?''

And when might that happen? 'Decades, I suppose. But I can imagine it coming.'

* The following correction was printed in the _Guardian_'s Corrections and clarifications column, Monday 15 March 2010:

Editing changes resulted in this article saying that the Government 'banned smoking in all enclosed public spaces in 2000, thereby securing a 25% drop in recorded numbers of smokers'. The story meant to say that the 2007 ban in England was an attempt to lock in the reduction in smokers registered since 2000. When it comes to Government figures for smokers, about 26.5% of the adult population smoked in 2000, falling to about 21% in 2008.

3 February 2010

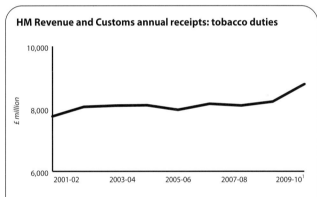

HM Revenue and Customs annual receipts: tobacco duties

£ million (y-axis: 6,000 to 10,000)

x-axis: 2001-02, 2003-04, 2005-06, 2007-08, 2009-10[1]

1. These figures are forecasts consistent with those published in the December 2009 pre-budget report. They fall outside the scope of National Statistics.

Source: Office for National Statistics/HM Revenue and Customs. Updated March 2010. Crown copyright.

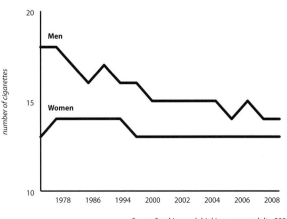

Average daily cigarette consumption per smoker by sex: 1974 to 2008. All aged 16 and over, Great Britain.

number of cigarettes (y-axis: 10 to 20)

Men
Women

x-axis: 1978, 1986, 1994, 2000, 2002, 2004, 2006, 2008

Source: Smoking and drinking among adults, 2008, Office for National Statistics. Crown copyright 2010.

THE GUARDIAN

Now they're giving up more than cigarettes

20 years after kicking the habit, spiked's editor-at-large Mick Hume bemoans the changed view of smokers and quitting.

The UK authorities have just made their usual pious New Year's resolution on our behalf: they resolve that we shall all give up smoking this year. Hence 2010 has begun as 2009 ended, with yet another round of state-sponsored anti-smoking propaganda, starring those all-singing TV adverts which insist that you should stop smoking for your kids, because they would 'do anything for you'. (These ads were presumably made by people without children.)

As one who has long been irritated by the increasingly shrill and illiberal anti-smoking crusade, I have been thinking again about the issue over the past week. Because this New Year marked the twentieth anniversary of the day I stopped smoking for good.

The intervening two decades have brought remarkable changes in the way that both smokers and giving up smoking are viewed in our society. It seems to me now that these changes are about far more than the way we see cigarettes. They mark a downward shift in the predominant cultural view of our humanity, and a demeaning of the qualities of adult autonomy and independence.

When I started smoking as a young teenager in the early 1970s, we all knew already that it was Very Bad for us. Those who imagine that bombarding youngsters with the terrible truth about smoking today will magically stop them taking it up are historically ignorant as well as naive. I recall being shown films of blackened smokers' lungs and wheezing old geezers in the primary school classrooms of the sixties. There was even an anti-smoking record, comprised largely of a hoarse smoker tunelessly coughing their guts out while promising to 'throw the packet away, away / when I've had just one more cigarette', which was played on the BBC's popular children's radio show *Junior Choice* every Saturday morning (I am not making this up).

None of this made any difference to us teenagers, of course, since smoking did not affect our young lungs like that. We smoked because we wanted to. Smoking was a statement about how you saw yourself – as grown-up, tough, cool, whatever – and an enjoyable social habit. Back then almost all of my mates smoked and the people I was attracted to tended to be smokers. Having got over the initial nausea of those first few cigarettes – you have always had to work hard to become a smoker – I loved everything about smoking, from the buzz to the look of it (I didn't realise it made me stink until I gave up, and of course none of my smoking friends noticed anyway). That

is, I loved everything about it except the price. At ten-and-a-half pence for ten of the cheapest fags when I started, we were hard pressed to afford a drag, and generally had to sacrifice a school dinner for the price of ten Player's Number Six. How young people find more than three quid for ten tax-hammered cigarettes today I have no idea – perhaps from parents who will do anything for them.

The mid-seventies marked the point at which the big decline in smoking in the UK began. But back then it was still seen as a normal, if slightly dirty habit. Smoking was legal even on the London Underground until after the King's Cross fire of 1987 (although anybody tempted to get nostalgic about the 'glamour' of the smoking age might like to recall those filthy Tube smoking carriages), and was accepted everywhere from buses to offices and of course pubs.

Importantly, whether or not you smoked was seen as your choice and your responsibility. Or as my ardently anti-smoking mother would say, 'It's your funeral' – and nobody else's. If you wanted to give up smoking, that was your choice and your problem too – other people would just shrug and wait to see how you got on, probably offering you a fag in the pub and expecting you to accept sooner or later.

In Britain in 1948, 82 per cent of men smoked some form of tobacco and 65 per cent were cigarette smokers

---

When I eventually stopped smoking at New Year 1990 it was certainly not because of being browbeaten about 'the children' or the planet – see latest propaganda about how smokers contribute to deforestation, etc. – or any of that. Like many people who decide to kick a habit, it was a personal decision made because something had changed in my own life. I turned 30 at the end of 1989, and had always foreseen that as a time to accept that one's body would start to lose the indestructible 'bouncebackability' of youth. My father and his brother had also quite recently died of smoking-related diseases in their fifties, as had their own father before them.

So like millions of others, I decided to pack it in and went cold turkey. In my case that meant going from 60 a day to none. In an age before nicotine patches and all that paraphernalia, I did it using the oral crutch of sucking 20-plus lollipops a day, which made me feel even sicker than the gut-wrenching withdrawal symptoms. The impact on

SPIKED

the UK tobacco industry was almost as harsh; I had always stayed loyal to No 6, although those strong little coffin nails had gone out of fashion, but a couple of months after a friend and I finally stopped smoking them Player's ceased manufacturing them. I still miss my beloved No 6, though I don't regret divorcing them.

In the 20 years since then I have watched two trends. On one hand a cultural shift has meant that smoking has become far less popular in Britain. According to Cancer Research, in Britain in 1948, when surveys of smoking began, 82 per cent of men smoked some form of tobacco and 65 per cent were cigarette smokers. By 1970, the percentage of cigarette smokers had fallen to 55 per cent. From the 1970s onwards, smoking prevalence fell rapidly. By 2007 around a fifth (22 per cent) of men (aged 16 and over) were reported as smokers – less than half the seventies rate. Between 1972 and 2007 the percentage of women who smoked also fell dramatically from 44 per cent to 20 per cent.

On the other hand, however, at the same time the anti-smoking campaign has become increasingly loud and authoritarian. The UK health authorities today talk about an 'epidemic' of smoking, which seems a strange way to refer to something that is not an illness and which anyway has more than halved in prevalence in recent decades. The past few years have brought bans on smoking in public places, and moves towards doing the same in private ones, alongside increasingly fierce anti-tobacco propaganda. Over Christmas I saw an old interview with John Mortimer, describing how finding himself alone in his wheelchair at a house party, while all the rest of the guests shivered and smoked in the back garden, struck him as the final proof that the country had gone mad.

Equally remarkable and surreal has been the change in attitudes and arguments used to justify this crackdown. Smoking is no longer seen as 'your funeral', an individual's problem. Instead it is has been redefined as anti-social behaviour, not simply something unpleasant to some but intolerable to all. The modern spectre of 'passive smoking' has been raised up as 'proof' that smokers are killing other people, especially children. In fact many health experts have acknowledged that the evidence for this is pretty thin, nothing compared to the hard evidence of the harm smokers do to themselves. But no matter. The case against passive smoking has been deployed to impose limits on anybody's freedom of choice about smoking.

This is a symptom of a wider cultural shift in which the illiberal authorities insist that you can no longer be allowed the right to make the 'wrong' choices about how you live. They have even invented a new political language to justify such interventions as being for our own good. As I noted when it first appeared alongside the smoking ban, the official unhyphenated word 'smokefree' fits pretty exactly George Orwell's description of a newspeak word created to turn 'freedom' into its opposite.

The move to redefine smoking as anti-social behaviour has also struck a chord with many because it chimes with the *cri de coeur* of the age – that your life is being messed up by other people, and you need protection from them (and possibly also from yourself). The underlying issue here is not passive smoking so much as passive living, inviting the authorities in to resolve your problems. Hence there was none of the talked-of resistance to the ban on smoking in public places. Where once it would have been thought these were matters for adults to sort out among themselves, now it is considered fair enough for the state forcibly to stub it out.

The flipside of the altered view of smokers is that giving up can no longer be left to those sorry individuals themselves. Nowadays, it seems, it takes a village to stop smoking. Since the habit of smoking tobacco is now deemed not just an addiction but almost to be a pathology, it must surely require therapy and psycho-medical intervention to 'cure' the sufferer.

Thus smokers are now inundated with offers of support groups and helplines and expert advice. The health authorities claim that these work, and no doubt they do for some who get involved. But the wider more worrying message is surely that it is too hard to give up on your own, that smokers are just too pathetic and spineless to cope with the pressures and side effects. Instead of deciding and acting for themselves, the only choice they need make is to be drawn into a therapeutic relationship with the state and its medical 'agents of persuasion', who will show the sinners how to repent and live a physically and spiritually healthy life. It almost sounds enough to drive any right-thinking individual back to the fag packet.

I don't regret stopping smoking 20 years ago, and it would be daft for anybody to take it up as some sort of political protest. But I do worry about what is behind the changed cultural status of smokers and giving up. I think I will always feel like a smoker inside, even though I hope never to have another puff. But even those who have never touched one should surely be concerned about the diminished view of adult autonomy and free choice that the anti-smoking crusade has helped to spread, opening the door to the new interfering 'politics of behaviour' in a way that would never have been tolerated in the smoke-filled rooms of yore.

Of course, having packed in smoking all those years ago, I have since become part of the 'overweight/obesity epidemic' that allegedly threatens us all today. As they used to say in another time: you pays your money and you takes your choice.

5 January 2010

SPIKED

Why are we punishing smokers?

Despite the Government's efforts, people keep smoking – so what does our eagerness to make them suffer say about us?

By Charlotte Gore

Andy Burnham has set himself the almighty challenge of halving the number of smokers, from a fifth of the population to a tenth. The hope is that this is like any other target – that with sufficient political will and enough public sector workers given the responsibility to turn the dream into a reality, anything can be accomplished. For the good of the state, a few individuals are going to have to change their ways.

I wonder whether Burnham understands the nature of the challenge he has undertaken for his Government on your behalf. The question is a significant one: is the state powerful enough to overcome an individual's extreme reluctance to part themselves from a substance addictive enough to have people plucking cigarette ends out of gutters in desperation?

How much humiliation, degradation and punishment is it necessary to inflict on a person before stopping smoking, with all the side effects and difficulties faced by those who do, becomes the path of least resistance? Smoking isn't a habit – it's a chemical dependency that causes changes in an individual's brain chemistry that are not easily – or quickly – reversed. It is an addiction with well-known long-term consequences that start with shortness of breath and end in premature, horrible, painful death.

Yet people continue to smoke. They stop when they want to stop, on their own terms, for their own reasons. Or they don't. They make the choice to continue doing something that is perfectly legal, in the full knowledge of the consequences and risks.

Considering all this, the proposal to ban smoking within a certain distance of doorways seems laughably inadequate. Pressure being brought to bear on individuals not to smoke in their cars or in their own homes goes a little further, but the original mission of protecting bar workers from the potential risks of passive smoking seems like a distant memory. The mission now is to rid smokers of their addiction for its own sake, and for the good of the state. The tools? Humiliation. Fear. Social stigmatisation. Isolation. Shame. Yet, for all their efforts, the addiction still wins out.

Perhaps it's possible for the Government to ramp up the pressure to the point where smokers can be literally terrorised into breaking their addiction against their will.

So this becomes a question for society: what level of terror are we willing to inflict on smokers in order to force them to stop? Is the goal really worth the oppression that would be required to have any real effect? And if the current level of official hostility against smokers is having no effect, what does it say about us that we support it irrespectively? Is it simply that expressing our displeasure at smokers makes people feel better about themselves?

> **Smoking remains legal, and raises a staggering £10bn every year for the treasury – more than four times what the NHS spends on smoking-related illnesses**

Still, all this misses the real issue. Smoking remains legal, and raises a staggering £10bn every year for the treasury – more than four times what the NHS spends on smoking-related illnesses. No matter what level of misery the Government inflicts on smokers through sanctions, controls, rules and propaganda, nothing compares to the suffering this level of taxation, often on the poorest in society – causes. This level of taxation can only happen because tobacco is addictive and the demand isn't influenced by price. If the Government quadrupled the price in one go that would be a serious shock that would impact demand – but they don't do it that way. The price creeps up so slowly that individuals don't notice how much more of their income is being extracted from them, until they realise it's taking it all, paying for £10bn-worth of public sector employees.

Then the cigarettes themselves cause more pain than any photograph of a corpse on a packet, or an advert on television giving smokers' children nightmares that their parents could die at any minute ever could. Caught in this triple hell of physical, financial and social suffering, smokers still keep smoking. It's staggering. It all simply goes away if they stop smoking, yet they do not. So what's it to be? Do you still want Burnham to push harder? What, exactly, does that say about you?

2 February 2010

THE GUARDIAN

Child tobacco pickers poisoned, reveals report

Information from Plan.

A new Plan report has revealed how child tobacco pickers in Malawi are being exposed to high levels of nicotine poisoning – the equivalent of 50 cigarettes per day.

'Hard work, little pay and long hours' documents how children as young as five are working up to 12 hours a day for as little as one penny an hour.

It is estimated that over 78,000 children work on tobacco estates across Malawi but Plan's research is thought to be the first with child pickers recording their own experiences.

Sick and abused

The children who took part in Plan's participatory research spoke about the need to work to support themselves, their families and pay school fees.

As well as physical and sexual abuse by their employers many were unknowingly showing classic signs of Green Tobacco Sickness (GTS).

Child tobacco pickers in Malawi are being exposed to high levels of nicotine poisoning – the equivalent of 50 cigarettes per day

This is a common and recognised hazard of workers absorbing nicotine through their skin by contact with moist tobacco leaves. There is a lack of research into long-term effects of GTS in children, but experts believe it could seriously impair their development.

Chest pains

The children reported symptoms including severe headaches, abdominal pain, muscle weakness, coughing and breathlessness.

'Sometimes it feels like you don't have enough breath, you don't have enough oxygen. You reach a point where you cannot breathe because of the pain in your chest. Then the blood comes when you vomit. At the end, most of this dies and then you remain with a headache,' one child said.

Malawi is the world's fifth biggest tobacco producer and the crop accounts for 70% of export income but despite the profits of multinational companies, local tobacco farmers continually struggle to break even.

This leads them to look for ways to cut costs with more children being exposed to hazardous and exploitative working conditions.

Corporate responsibility

Plan is now calling upon tobacco companies and plantations to vastly improve working conditions and live up to their own promised corporate responsibility guidelines by scrutinising their suppliers far more closely.

They should provide safe environments and non-exploitative wages and access to education for those children who have to work.

Plan also wants the government of Malawi to rigorously enforce existing child labour and protection laws and review land inheritance laws which restrict families' ownership of land.

24 August 2009

⇨ The above information is reprinted with kind permission from Plan. Visit www.plan-international. org for more information. Founded more than 70 years ago, Plan is one of the oldest and largest development organisations in the world. Plan is a global organisation, working in 66 countries, and is completely independent, with no religious, political or governmental affiliations. Plan works to promote children's rights in order to end child poverty, guided by the United Nations Conventions on the Rights of the Child.

© *Plan*

PLAN

⇨ The prevalence of cigarette smoking fell substantially in the 1970s and the early 1980s, from 45 per cent in 1974 to 35 per cent in 1982. The rate of decline then slowed. (page 1)

⇨ About two-thirds of respondents who were either current smokers or who had smoked regularly at some time in their lives had started smoking before they were 18. (page 3)

⇨ Every year, around 114,000 smokers in the UK die from smoking-related causes. About half of all regular cigarette smokers will eventually be killed by their addiction. (page 4)

⇨ Cigarette smoke contains many substances which can damage the lungs. The smoke has two parts: tiny solid pieces which contain tar, and the gas, which contains carbon monoxide and nitrogen oxides. Smoking takes these poisonous substances directly into your lungs. (page 5)

⇨ Chemicals in cigarette smoke can damage the lining of the coronary arteries. This leads to atherosclerosis – the build-up of fatty material within the walls of the arteries which is the cause of coronary heart disease. (page 7)

⇨ Experts agree that smoking is the single biggest cause of cancer in the world. Smoking causes over a quarter of cancer deaths in developed countries. (page 8)

⇨ The Royal College of Physicians compared nicotine to other supposedly 'harder' drugs. The panel concluded that nicotine causes addiction in much the same way as heroin or cocaine and is just as addictive, if not more so, than these 'harder' drugs. (page 10)

⇨ Smoking 20 a day for a year costs £1,825. (page 13)

⇨ 41% of men and 37% of women who are or had ever been regular smokers started smoking before they were 16. (page 13)

⇨ There are 43 elements contained in cigarettes that have been found to cause cancer. (page 15)

⇨ Scientists found that rich smokers were more likely to die young than non-smokers from the least affluent backgrounds. Smoking also all but eradicated the traditional advantage in longevity that women enjoy over men. (page 18)

⇨ Roll-your-own (RYO) cigarettes expose smokers to similar levels of cancer-causing chemicals as manufactured cigarettes according to a new study. (page 19)

⇨ Research reveals that tobacco products bearing the word 'smooth' or using lighter coloured branding mislead people into thinking that these products are less harmful to their health. (page 20)

⇨ Research commissioned by ASH has shown that the cost to the NHS of treating diseases caused by smoking is approximately £2.7 billion a year. (page 22)

⇨ A young person's immediate social environment – especially the smoking behaviour and attitudes of significant others – has an important influence. Smoking by parents, siblings, and friends and peers are all important predictors of tobacco use. (page 24)

⇨ Young people choose to smoke for their own personal desire and curiosity rather than because of the traditional concept of being forced into conforming with friends' behaviour, a new study highlights. (page 27)

⇨ According to a study, smokers who are continually confronted with warnings that cigarettes kill actually develop coping mechanisms to justify continuing their habit. (page 29)

⇨ One in four (28%) pregnant smokers would like to seek help to stop smoking but are worried about being judged. (page 30)

⇨ 62% of men and 64% of women who smoke 20 or more cigarettes a day would like to give up smoking altogether. (page 32)

⇨ Yorkshire has the greatest regional concentration of smokers, at 25% of the population. (page 33)

⇨ 14% of pregnant women continue to smoke. (page 33)

⇨ A new Plan report has revealed how child tobacco pickers in Malawi are being exposed to high levels of nicotine poisoning – the equivalent of 50 cigarettes per day. (page 39)

Acetone

Widely used as a solvent, for example in nail polish remover, acetone is one of around 4,000 chemicals contained in the average cigarette.

Ammonia

A chemical found in cleaning fluids, ammonia is inhaled during smoking.

Arsenic

A deadly poison used in insecticides, arsenic is contained in tobacco and is therefore inhaled during smoking.

Cadmium

A metal used in batteries, also contained in tobacco.

Cigarette

A paper tube filled with tobacco which is lit at one end and inhaled orally (smoked). There are many slang words for cigarettes, including fags, tabs, smokes and cigs/ciggies. Cigarettes can be bought pre-prepared or hand-rolled. Most modern cigarettes contain a spongy filter which reduces the amount of poisonous chemicals inhaled while smoking: however, a large part of these substances is still absorbed and smoking therefore poses a substantial health risk.

Tobacco can also be inhaled using cigars and pipes, or it can be chewed. There are health risks associated with all methods of inhaling tobacco.

Carbon monoxide

A toxic gas released when something is burnt incompletely, found in tobacco smoke.

Cyanide

A poisonous compound, found in tobacco smoke.

Formaldehyde

A chemical used to preserve corpses. Formaldehyde is contained in tobacco.

Nicotine

An addictive chemical compound found in the nightshade family of plants that makes up about 0.6–3.0% of dry weight of tobacco. It is the nicotine contained in tobacco which causes smokers to become addicted, and many will use Nicotine Replacement Therapy such as patches, gum or electronic cigarettes to help them deal with cravings while quitting.

Passive smoking

Passive smoking refers to the inhalation of tobacco smoke by someone other than the smoker: for example, a parent smoking near their children may expose them to the poisonous chemicals in the second-hand smoke from their cigarette. This has been shown to have a negative impact on the passive smoker's health.

The smoking ban

The Health Act 2006, which came into force in England and Wales on 1 July 2007, made it illegal to smoke in all enclosed public places and enclosed work places (similar bans were already in place in other parts of the UK). This has led to much debate about the balance between public health and individual freedoms.

Tar

A mixture of chemicals (including formaldehyde, arsenic and cyanide). About 70 per cent of the tar in a cigarette is left in smokers' lungs, causing a range of serious lung conditions.

Tobacco

Tobacco is a brown herb-like substance produced from the dried leaves of tobacco plants. The tobacco used in cigarettes contains many substances dangerous to the user when inhaled, including tar, which can cause lung cancer, and nicotine, which is highly addictive. Nevertheless, around 21 per cent of adults in the UK are smokers.

Tobacco duty

An abbreviation of tobacco products duty, it is a type of tax charged on purchases of tobacco products.

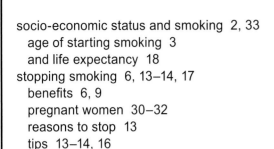

Additional Resources

Other Issues titles

If you are interested in researching further some of the issues raised in *Tobacco and Health,* you may like to read the following titles in the **Issues** series:

⇨ Vol. 187 *Health and the State* (ISBN 978 1 86168 528 5)

⇨ Vol. 186 *Cannabis Use* (ISBN 978 1 86168 527 8)

⇨ Vol. 176 *Health Issues for Young People* (ISBN 978 1 86168 500 1)

⇨ Vol. 163 *Drugs in the UK* (ISBN 978 1 86168 456 1)

⇨ Vol. 162 *Staying Fit* (ISBN 978 1 86168 455 4)

⇨ Vol. 143 *Problem Drinking* (ISBN 978 1 86168 409 7)

For a complete list of available **Issues** titles, please visit our website: www.independence.co.uk/shop

Useful organisations

You may find the websites of the following organisations useful for further research:

⇨ **Addiction:** www.addictionjournal.org

⇨ **ASH:** www.ash.org.uk

⇨ **British Heart Foundation:** www.bhf.org.uk

⇨ **British Lung Foundation:** www.lunguk.org

⇨ **British Medical Association:** www.bma.org.uk

⇨ **British Psychological Society:** www.bps.org.uk

⇨ **Cancer Research UK:** www.cancerresearchuk.org

⇨ **Centre for Public Health:** www.cph.org.uk

⇨ **Hope UK:** www.hopeuk.org

⇨ **Medical News Today:** www.medicalnewstoday.com

⇨ **NHS Choices:** www.nhs.uk

⇨ **Smokefree NHS:** http://smokefree.nhs.uk

For more book information, visit our website...

www.independence.co.uk

Information available online includes:

✓ Detailed descriptions of titles

✓ Tables of contents

✓ Facts and figures

✓ Online ordering facilities

✓ Log-in page for Issues Online (an Internet resource available free to Firm Order Issues subscribers – ask your librarian to find out if this service is available to you)

ACKNOWLEDGEMENTS

The publisher is grateful for permission to reproduce the following material.

While every care has been taken to trace and acknowledge copyright, the publisher tenders its apology for any accidental infringement or where copyright has proved untraceable. The publisher would be pleased to come to a suitable arrangement in any such case with the rightful owner.

Chapter One: Smoking and Health

Smoking among adults, 2008, © Crown copyright is reproduced with the permission of Her Majesty's Stationery Office, *Tobacco,* © Hope UK, *Smoking and your lungs,* © British Lung Foundation, *Prevalence of cigarette smoking by age [graph],* © Crown copyright is reproduced with the permission of Her Majesty's Stationery Office, *Smoking and your heart,* © British Heart Foundation, *Tobacco, smoking and cancer: the evidence,* © Cancer Research UK, *Smokers putting their loved ones at risk of heart attacks,* © Addiction, *Under-18s guide to quitting,* © Crown copyright is reproduced with the permission of Her Majesty's Stationery Office, *Age started smoking regularly by sex, 2008 [graphs],* © Crown copyright is reproduced with the permission of Her Majesty's Stationery Office, *Attitudes of young smokers,* © British Psychological Society, *Up in smoke!,* © Student UK, *How do I stop making excuses not to quit?,* © Crown copyright is reproduced with the permission of Her Majesty's Stationery Office, *Most ex-smokers quit successfully without help,* © Medical News Today, *Smoking 'worse for your health than being working class',* © Telegraph Media Group Ltd 2010, *Roll-your-own cigarettes as deadly as ready-mades,* © Cancer Research UK, *Type of cigarette smoked by age and sex [graphs],* © Crown copyright is reproduced with the permission of Her Majesty's Stationery Office, *Cigarette pack design gives misleading smoke signals,* © ASH, *'More research' needed into safety of electronic cigarettes,* © Cancer Research UK.

Chapter Two: Smoking and Society

The economics of tobacco, © ASH, *Forever cool: the influence of smoking imagery on young people,* © British Medical Association, *Teenage smoking: it's my choice not yours,* © Centre for Public Health,

Cigarette-smoking status by age, Percentage who have never smoked cigarettes regularly by sex [graphs], © Crown copyright is reproduced with the permission of Her Majesty's Stationery Office, *Cigarette pack health warnings 'could encourage people to keep smoking',* © Telegraph Media Group Ltd 2010, *Social stigma prevents pregnant smokers seeking help to quit,* © Crown copyright is reproduced with the permission of Her Majesty's Stationery Office, *Proportion of smokers who would like to give up smoking altogether [graphs],* © Crown copyright is reproduced with the permission of Her Majesty's Stationery Office, *War on smokers: the backlash,* © Guardian News and Media Limited 2010, *HM Revenue and Customs annual receipts: tobacco duties, Average daily cigarette consumption per smoker by sex [graphs],* © Crown copyright is reproduced with the permission of Her Majesty's Stationery Office, *Now they're giving up more than cigarettes,* © spiked, *Why are we punishing smokers?,* © Guardian News and Media Limited 2010, *Child tobacco pickers poisoned, reveals report,* © Plan.

Illustrations

Pages 2, 11, 18, 29: Don Hatcher; pages 4, 12: Bev Aisbett; pages 5, 16, 20, 39: Angelo Madrid; pages 7, 15, 27, 31: Simon Kneebone.

Cover photography

Left: © Arjen Doting, Adres. Centre: © Adam Ciesielski. Right: © Jenny Rollo.

Additional acknowledgements

Research by Robert Fletcher.

Additional research by Hart McLeod Limited, Cambridge.

And with thanks to the Independence team: Mary Chapman, Sandra Dennis and Jan Sunderland.

Lisa Firth
Cambridge
May, 2010